→INTRODUCING

SOCIOLOGY

JOHN NAGLE & PIERO

This edition published in
the UK and the USA in 2016
by Icon Books Ltd,
39-41 North Road, London N7 9DP
info@iconbooks.com
www.introducingbooks.com

Sold in the UK, Europe and Asia
by Faber & Faber Ltd,
Bloomsbury House,
74–77 Great Russell Street,
London WC1B 3DA or their agents

Distributed in the UK, Europe and
Asia by Grantham Book Services,
Trent Road, Grantham, NG31 7XQ

Distributed in South Africa
by Jonathan Ball, Office B4,
The District, 41 Sir Lowry Road,
Woodstock 7925

Distributed in Australia and
New Zealand by Allen & Unwin Pty
Ltd, PO Box 8500, 83 Alexander
Street, Crows Nest, NSW 2065

Distributed in the USA
by Publishers Group West
1700 Fourth Street
Berkeley, CA 94710

Distributed in Canada
by Publishers Group Canada,
76 Stafford Street, Unit 300,
Toronto, Ontario M6J 2S1

Distributed in India
by Penguin Books India, 7th Floor,
Infinity Tower – C, DLF Cyber City,
Gurgaon 122002, Haryana

ISBN: 978-178578-073-8

Text and illustrations copyright © 2016 Icon Books Ltd

The author and artist have asserted their moral rights.

Editor: Kiera Jamison

Printed and bound in the UK by Clays Ltd, St Ives plc

Kung Fu Sociology

In a documentary on the life and work of the leading sociologist **Pierre Bourdieu** (1930–2002), Bourdieu explains that "sociology is a martial art". Bourdieu is not suggesting that learning sociology will automatically qualify the student for a black belt in Kung Fu. Instead, he sees the value of sociology as helping to "unmask domination": forms of social inequality based on class, race, gender and much more besides. Despite the existence of domination in our everyday lives, it is often disguised so that we fail to recognize it. For Bourdieu, the role of sociology is to expose the workings of domination throughout our societies.

This book is not intended to be some sort of self-help guide or instruction manual that equips the reader with the tools to transform their societies. A rather more modest proposal is suggested. By outlining key sociological thinkers, concepts and ideas, the objective is to familiarize the reader with the rich intellectual heritage of the discipline. Although, if, as Bourdieu supposed, an engagement with sociology is akin to learning a combat sport, reading this book may provide you with some of the training required to build a just and fair society.

No Such Thing as Society?

In a 1987 interview, the then UK Prime Minister **Margaret Thatcher** (1925–2013) famously stated:

> THERE'S NO SUCH THING AS SOCIETY.

A sociologist would both agree and disagree with Thatcher's sentiments about society. However much humans appear to exhibit "individual" behaviour and live in a world of incredible choice, our access to choice is limited by the social groups we are members of. They may agree with Thatcher, however, that society does not exist as an unchanging and fixed set of institutions.

> OUR VALUES AND OPPORTUNITIES ARE FORMED BY OUR POSITION WITHIN SOCIETY. SOCIETY IS ALSO THE SUM OF EVERYDAY INTERACTIONS BETWEEN PEOPLE SEEKING TO ATTAIN COMMON AIMS.

What Is Sociology?

Is it possible to provide a simple definition of sociology? This task appears especially difficult when we consider that the discipline of sociology is now over a century old and contains a wide range of theoretical and methodological approaches. One way to consider sociology is as a methodical study of the ways that people are affected by and affect society, and the processes that are associated with groups, societies and institutions.

GOOD SOCIOLOGY IS SOCIOLOGICAL WORK THAT PRODUCES MEANINGFUL DESCRIPTIONS OF ORGANIZATIONS AND EVENTS, VALID EXPLANATIONS OF HOW THEY COME ABOUT AND PERSIST, AND REALISTIC PROPOSALS FOR THEIR IMPROVEMENT OR REMOVAL.

Howard Becker, b. 1928

The aim or perspective of sociology is to reveal how social structures create both opportunities and constraints that characterize our lives.

Social structures are those relatively stable relationships between people that are shaped by institutions. Sociology maps out social structures so we can begin to see the social forces that act upon us.

By challenging the myth that human behaviour is purely individualistic or driven by biological impulses, sociology encourages us to understand the social dynamics that turn us into members of society.

The Sociological Imagination

Thinking sociologically is what the American sociologist **C. Wright Mills** (1916–62) termed the "sociological imagination". Mills said that when we develop a sociological imagination we begin to see how wider social forces connect with our personal biographies. For Mills, the sociological imagination is particularly powerful when we identify the society we live in, rather any personal or individual failings, as responsible for many of our problems.

MY STRUGGLE TO PAY THE RENT IS CONNECTED TO GOVERNMENT POLICIES ON MINIMUM WAGE AND EMPLOYMENT LAW.

Mills recognized that cultivating the sociological imagination is not easy. It is far too easy to blame laziness for unemployment and fecklessness for poverty. Equally, it is too easy to single out individual intelligence when a student lands a place at a top university. Yet the sociological imagination compels us to see racial, gender and socioeconomic inequalities not as facts of nature but as products of the social world.

Public Sociology

Nurturing a sociological imagination is the first step towards a public sociology. A public sociology, as the phrase suggests, is concerned with making the public into more engaged citizens. This is a sociology that is not limited to academia – it aims to lead public policy. Sociology has an ingrained public purpose. By explaining to us about how society functions, many sociologists, such as **Zygmunt Bauman** (b.1925), hope that we will seek to change it in some way that makes for a fairer world. By thinking sociologically, we may well see the social context of our lives that has previously been obscured, and learn that we are not simply prisoners of the social structure.

THE MORE WE GRASP HOW THE WHEELS OF THE SYSTEM ARE OPERATED, THE MORE POWER WE HAVE TO RESIST AND EVEN FREE OURSELVES FROM IT.

It can seem as though sociologists have a very pessimistic view of society. This is not necessarily true. Sociologists recognize that humans are social creatures and that when we cooperate this can lead to strong public institutions and a fair society. Yet, sociologists concede that our societies typically contain forms of inequality, stratification and discrimination, and this is not natural. Where this is the case, sociologists believe that we as individuals and members of social groups can change our conditions.

Puppets and Dangerous Giants

Peter Berger (b.1929) compares the social world to a puppet theatre. We may appear to be puppets with roles that are seemingly determined by the invisible strings of society and the puppet-master hidden from view. But, as we pick up the rules of the theatre and our prescribed parts as actors, we see the mechanisms that allow the theatre to operate.

Erving Goffman (1922–82) also recognized the potential of sociology to make individuals into "dangerous giants" with the strength to tear down the structures they are imprisoned within.

Origins and Birth of Sociology

If sociology is the study of social forces, what sort of social, political and intellectual ideas and traditions gave birth to sociology? Sociology emerged within the matrix of massive social, political and intellectual change in the late 18th and early 19th centuries.

Over the next 17 pages, we'll trace the development of the field of sociology.

Let's begin with the intellectual ideas that nourished sociology. A good starting point is the **Enlightenment**, an age of unprecedented intellectual advance and political awakening in the 18th century. The Enlightenment was propelled by radical thinkers who applied science and rationalism, rather than religion and superstition, to explain the world. Some of these scholars provided a formative scientific perspective on social life: a science of society should look for rational causes for social phenomena rather than theological or metaphysical ones.

THE HUMAN MIND IS A BLANK SLATE, NOT SHAPED BY GOD BUT BY EXPERIENCE!

John Locke
(1632–1704)

Hegel and the Spirit

The German philosopher **G.W. Hegel** (1770–1831) sketched an "idealist" theory of society and history in which society is imagined as having a spirit. He envisaged the spirit not as a social force but as a manifestation of the divine, which is why, although Hegel's thinking is revolutionary, it is not quite sociology.

THE SPIRIT OF SOCIETY AND ITS CULTURE FORMS THE SUBJECTIVE IDEAS WHICH MAKE US ACT.

Hegel mapped out history as a slow and painful transformation from local to global institutions. It is the formation of the **nation-state** that he saw as the important social institution, since it is here where the spirit of society and the people are contained. Hegel's contribution to the development of sociology is that he begins to analyse the role of social institutions – religious and government – in bringing about social change and reform.

Sociology was borne out of bewildering social and political transformation shaped by the two major revolutions of the era – the French and Industrial revolutions. These twins all but dissolved existing forms of social organization in Europe. **The French Revolution** (1789–99), which witnessed the overthrow of a monarchical dynasty, generated new and radical ideas about the state, the role of religion in social life, and political and social reform. Driven by scientific discoveries and technological advances, the **Industrial Revolution** created a factory-based, capitalist economy during the 19th century.

New forms of social stratification emerged as a consequence, and the growth of the industrial city provided a new historical stage for complex forms of social organization, especially the development of socioeconomic classes.

Set against the turmoil of unprecedented political and social change, early sociological thinkers aimed to explain the forces that had created industrial society, and asked important questions that gave the discipline its identity. To address these questions entailed asking a range of further questions. While early sociological theorists all posed variations of the same questions, they often disagreed on the answers.

Auguste Comte – Sociology Finds a Name

The figure commonly credited with laying down the intellectual foundations of the discipline is **Auguste Comte** (1798–1857). In 1839 Comte created the word "sociology" to describe his ideas. Deeply influenced and inspired by science, Comte wished to provide a scientific explanation of society and he applied "**positivism**" as his main approach. Positivism is the study of observable phenomena as a means to analyse society.

Comte believed that rational thought married to the use of hard evidence could advance human understanding on how societies successfully function and why they go through historical change.

Auguste Comte

IF I APPLY LOGICAL THOUGHT TO MY OBSERVATIONS OF THE WORLD, I CAN ARRIVE AT A BETTER UNDERSTANDING OF SOCIETY.

Statics and Dynamics

On the topic of how societies both function and change, Comte coined two related terms – "social statics" and "social dynamics".

Social statics are principles concerning the connection between and coexistence of institutions that allow society to function relatively smoothly and harmoniously. Society is seen as a complex system that simultaneously operates as a cohesive and integrated structure. The key ingredient that keeps society together is institutions – such as family and religion – which function as part of a whole, rather than as isolated and individual components.

Social dynamics attends to how social institutions change over time to create social transformation. The flow of information around social institutions changes these structures in different ways, and this creates human progress.

Comte believed that healthy social systems are characterized by harmony between different types of institutions. A key institution in maintaining societal balance is the "**division of labour**" – how people organize production and satisfy their material needs. **Language** is also an important social glue. Language allows group members to communicate and pass on values and knowledge. **Religion**, finally, achieves a common sense of purpose for people.

ALL OF THESE INSTITUTIONS COMBINE TO FORM A SOCIAL STRUCTURE THAT MAINTAINS SOLIDARITY FOR MEMBERS OF SOCIETY.

Comte also believed that sociology would be one engine of human progress to lead us to utopia, a world in which science and rationalism would emancipate us from superstition and blind faith. Comte outlined his famous "**law of three stages**" of world history: three successive stages, each of which contains specific social institutions. The final stage, the "Positive", is the emergence of what Comte coined "industrial society".

THE POSITIVE STAGE WILL FINALLY MATURE INTO UTOPIA.

Comte realized that the coming of industrial society would create new political and social crises. But his faith in scientific progress made him argue that such problems would be resolved in a new rational system. European society would require reconstruction around the values of science and rationality. The act of reconstruction required the creation of a "Religion of Humanity", a secular religion dedicated to progress. Sociologists were the new priestly caste of his religion.

Spencer and Social Evolution

Comte's influence is most heavily felt in the work of **Herbert Spencer** (1820–1903), who adopted Comte's concept of social statics and social dynamics. Spencer went further than Comte in viewing a "functionalist" concept of society, in which each part of society specializes around a specific function or purpose.

Attempting to account for social change in his functionalist model, Spencer somewhat misappropriated Charles Darwin's work on evolution, in combination with Comte's ideas. He adapted social dynamics to "social evolution", which involved both "**structural differentiation**" (how apparently "simple'" societies became increasingly complex) and "**functional adaptation**" (how societies adjust to change and complex forms of social organization).

While Charles Darwin defined "fitness" as reproductive success, Spencer believed that survival of the fittest relates to those institutional forms best equipped to flourish in their society.

THIS SURVIVAL OF THE FITTEST, WHICH I HAVE EXPRESSED IN MECHANICAL TERMS, IS THAT WHICH MR DARWIN CALLED "NATURAL SELECTION", OR THE PRESERVATION OF FAVOURED RACES IN THE STRUGGLE FOR LIFE.

Karl Marx – Conflict and Revolution

Comte and Spencer both believed that social systems create harmony and stability in an age of industrial society. Many sociological thinkers of the 19th and early 20th centuries did not share this view. On the contrary, they saw conflict and division as typical features of society. The radical German thinker **Karl Marx** (1818–83) is one of these; although he never described his work as sociology, he thought sociologically and inspired generations of sociological research.

In some ways, Marx shared Comte and Spencer's belief in historical change and progress. But his work sought to show that history – and not just industrial society – was propelled forward by conflict between different social classes over values and resources. Marx described this as "**historical materialism**". It is the mode of production that decides the overall economic, social and political institutions of any given society. Each society is defined by a mode of production that the competing social classes fight to control in order to advance their own interests. Marx believed that the industrial working class would win this struggle between classes and this would lead to a communist society.

THE HISTORY OF ALL HITHERTO EXISTING SOCIETIES HAS BEEN THE HISTORY OF CLASS STRUGGLES.

Marx noted that while all societies have social institutions, it is the economic structure that shapes these institutions. A society's economic system provides the base or social infrastructure, which shapes not only political, legal and customary social institutions, but also consciousness and knowledge. Ideas and ideologies are by formed by material conditions.

IT IS NOT THE CONSCIOUSNESS OF MEN THAT DETERMINES THEIR BEING, BUT, ON THE CONTRARY, THEIR SOCIAL BEING THAT DETERMINES THEIR CONSCIOUSNESS.

Social Conflict

Two central themes to Marx's work are critical to the development of sociology. First, his analysis of social conflict as the engine of historical change brings the concept of **social class** into the discipline. In the industrial age, Marx described the conflict between two social classes: the dominant and oppressed, or the bourgeoisie (rulers and factory owners) and the proletariat (factory workers).

In this monumental clash, Marx predicted the ultimate victory of the workers who would overcome oppression through revolutionary class action. The fruit of victory would be the arrival of communism. Although Marx never specified the details of communist society, it was egalitarian, with the workers controlling the means of production.

LET THE RULING CLASSES TREMBLE AT A COMMUNIST REVOLUTION. THE PROLETARIANS HAVE NOTHING TO LOSE BUT THEIR CHAINS.

Secondly, Marx introduced the idea of "**alienation**", the experience of isolation resulting from powerlessness. In the mechanized industrial system, Marx argued that capitalism alienated ordinary factory workers from the act of work, from the products they made, from their fellow workers, and even from human potential itself.

Alienation resulted from individuals belonging to social classes, particularly the working class, and was thus a product of the capitalist system. As such, the capitalist class – the owners of factories – benefitted from the power that alienation had over the workers. Although it took many forms, a key form of alienation occurred when workers competed with each other for jobs and salaries.

Through his radical writings, Marx laid the ground for a public sociology in which sociologists are instrumental actors in achieving revolutionary transformation. The point of research and the collection of knowledge is that we can use it to challenge the power of capitalists and the society they have built, and to create a world free of socioeconomic inequalities. From then on, research should take the perspective of the working class.

THE PHILOSOPHERS HAVE ONLY INTERPRETED THE WORLD, IN VARIOUS WAYS. THE POINT, HOWEVER, IS TO CHANGE IT.

If the "sociological imagination" is to make us aware of how personal problems are linked to massive social forces, Marx called for radical thinkers to challenge "**false consciousness**": the state of mind in which shortcomings are classified as the product of the individual rather than the flaws of capitalist society.

Once we begin to understand our relationship to the mode of production and thus society, the first step towards challenging the system has been made. Marx wanted us to develop a "**class consciousness**", an awareness of how we are exploited.

Durkheim – The Discipline Develops

Alongside Marx, other seminal thinkers began to lay the foundations for sociology. The French researcher **Émile Durkheim** (1858–1917) was influenced by Comte's faith in the application of scientific method to understand the social world. Durkheim wanted to prove that the discipline of sociology had a rightful place in universities beside science. In 1895, he founded the first university sociology department.

Durkheim's scientific sociology was motivated by his belief, like Marx, that modern industrial society had extremely harmful consequences for many individuals. However, his response to industrial society differed from Marx's in important ways.

CONFLICT AND DIVISION ARE THE MAIN CHARACTERISTICS OF MODERN SOCIETY. THE END POINT OF HUMAN PROGRESS IS REVOLUTION AND COMMUNISM. WE MUST TAKE THE PERSPECTIVE OF THE WORKING CLASS.

Émile Durkheim

SOLIDARITY IS CRUCIAL TO KEEP SOCIETY TOGETHER. SOCIOLOGY CAN HELP TO ACHIEVE GRADUAL SOCIAL REFORM. WE MUST TAKE A NEUTRAL AND SCIENTIFIC ANALYSIS.

Solidarity

Central to Durkheim's sociology is the idea that patterns of human behaviour form established structures and institutions. Society is a complex organism which represents more than the sum of its parts. Durkheim asked how this organism functions in industrial society. He responded by analysing the division of labour. The division of labour in relatively small traditional societies is defined by "**mechanical solidarity**": a strong sense of communal unity maintained by a system of shared beliefs and morality.

The advent of industrial society created a new division of labour typified by "**organic solidarity**". Organic solidarity is where social relationships are based on specific forms of specialization that unite members.

While small-scale societies are kept together by a moral consensus shared by group members, modern industrial society works through functional interdependence.

Social Facts

So, social norms are vital to keep society functioning. But how do we know what they are?

HOW WE THINK, FEEL AND ACT IS A DIRECT CONSEQUENCE OF THE SOCIETY THAT NOURISHES US.

Durkheim called the experience of norms, values and religious beliefs that lie outside of each person and exist as part of wider society "social facts". When we perform social roles and obligations, we usually do so without questioning why. These social roles become almost second nature. They consist of manners of acting, thinking and feeling that are invested with a power by virtue of which they exercise control over us. In making social facts the main object of sociological investigation, Durkheim distinguishes the discipline of sociology from the sciences, which are concerned with the natural world.

Crime

The investigation of social facts reveals how social structure guides human actions and values. Social facts demonstrate that individual behaviour is largely the result of social structures; these "facts" are therefore central to how society functions and solidarity is maintained.

Paradoxically, even the act of crime has an essential role in maintaining social order. Durkheim understood crime in industrial society as being partly a result of weakening societal bonds, caused by the growth of industrial society. Durkheim was interested in how the act of crime is used to *confirm* social morality. Crime is defined as such because it breaks social rules.

CRIME IS AN ACT OF DEVIANCY THAT HIGHLIGHTS THE VERY POWER OF SOCIAL NORMS. WE DO NOT CONDEMN IT BECAUSE IT IS A CRIME, BUT IT IS A CRIME BECAUSE WE CONDEMN IT.

Suicide

Durkheim originated a methodological approach for sociological study, which he set out in a book published in 1897 on suicide. His methodology relied on the compilation and analysis of statistics. Rather than the result of individual illness, Durkheim hypothesized that suicide had social causes, and he proceeded to collect data to support his theory. Through scrupulous attention to statistics of suicide rates among different social groups, within different countries, and over a period of time, Durkheim noted that while the rate of suicide was relatively consistent within each country, there were notable differences between countries. There was a greater prevalence of suicide among Protestants compared to Catholics; suicide rates were higher not only in Protestant compared to Catholic countries, but between Protestants and Catholics in the same country.

Simply establishing an association between suicide and religious groups was not enough. Durkheim explained differences in suicide levels in terms of Catholics having a stronger sense of social control and living in more integrated communities, compared to the more individualistic Protestants. His research revealed a further range of societal factors for suicide: increased rates associated with sudden economic change, or being single and not having children, and decreased rates associated with living in wartime (regardless of whether your country is winning or losing).

Durkheim's research demonstrates that **social solidarity** is the overall explanatory feature. Individuals who feel isolated from their social communities are vulnerable to suicide. In a modern society defined by individualism and a lack of traditional authority, suicide is particularly apparent.

Max Weber

Another major figure of early sociology is **Max Weber** (1864–1920). Weber differed from Durkheim on social facts, particularly on how we should analyse them. He argued that observation is worthless without first having underlying concepts about how the social world works. As part of this, Weber stated that social scientists have a responsibility to acknowledge the existence of their individual biases when it comes to conducting research. It is natural for sociologists to assign moral values to the social world, meaning that "value-free" research is difficult.

SOCIOLOGISTS SHOULD AIM FOR VALUE NEUTRALITY IN THEIR RESEARCH. WE SHOULD REMOVE OUR IDEOLOGICAL, CULTURAL AND NON-SCIENTIFIC ASSUMPTIONS FROM RESEARCH. BUT CAN WE EVER BE TRULY OBJECTIVE AND NEUTRAL WHEN WE DO RESEARCH ON THE SOCIAL WORLD?

The Ideal Type

It is simply not possible in sociological research to fully capture the diversity and complexity of social action. Instead, sociologists generalize results, comparing and contrasting social phenomena across periods of time and geographical locations. How do they do this? Weber believed that sociologists should utilize an "ideal type". The ideal type is a constructed ideal used to approximate reality by selecting and accentuating certain elements.

Weber's ideal type is to look for the essential, though slightly exaggerated, characteristics of social life. Weber asks us to consider, for example, the ideal type of capitalist society, Protestant women or even civil war. Through identifying the key facets of the type, we can conduct systematic research.

Weber's main intellectual contribution to sociology stems from his writings on the transformation of societies based on tradition to those characterized by "rationality". When societies transform into industrial capitalist systems, they inevitably experience "disenchantment" and an increase in rationalization as the dominant mode of thought.

Disenchantment refers to the erosion of all mystery and spontaneity from modern life. Weber claims that the modern world's obsession with efficiency and rational control of all aspects of the social world will eventually trap us in an "iron cage". The iron cage, stated Weber, is the effect of living in a bureaucratic society based on rational calculation.

Protestant Work Ethic and Capitalism

Weber argued that the fundamental cause of the rationalization of modern society was the emergence of capitalism, and he tracked the values and ideas that drove the long-term genesis of modern capitalism from the Protestant Reformation to the modern day.

Central to the story is the cultivation of particular cultural values that lend themselves to capitalism. Weber claims that the spirit of capitalism is particularly evident with Protestantism and its "work ethic": there is an "elective affinity" between Protestant theology and the worldview of capitalism. Weber's analysis of Protestant theology demonstrates how cultural values – like religion – can be instrumental in major social change.

WHY DID CAPITALISM DEVELOP FIRST IN WESTERN EUROPE? WHILE MARX SAW RELIGION AS BASED IN ECONOMIC PROCESSES, I BELIEVE THAT RELIGION CAN INDEPENDENTLY FOSTER ECONOMIC STRUCTURES.

The "Protestant work ethic" drives the beginnings of capitalist society. Capitalism is seen to occur first in countries where the Protestant Reformation was successful. Some Protestant sects see individual economic wealth as a sign of God's grace. They therefore apply rationality, hard work and self-denial to accumulate money. The spirit urges people to see excessive spending as immoral and to be rejected, so financial wealth is reinvested to generate even greater profit.

The Protestant work ethic is founded on an **ascetic** lifestyle, which involves hard work, discipline, frugality and a rational approach to using time.

The ascetic Protestant lifestyle also involves other kinds of self-control. Sexuality is viewed as dangerous as it arouses bodily pleasure and leads to a loss of self-control. The function of sex is seen as reproduction, not enjoyment. Overeating is also condemned, viewed as evidence of a lack of control. The Protestant work ethic becomes the central principle of life in capitalist countries, regardless of whether the population is Protestant or not.

WE ARE DEALING WITH THE CONNECTION OF THE SPIRIT OF MODERN ECONOMIC LIFE WITH THE RATIONAL ETHICS OF ASCETIC PROTESTANTISM.

The Iron Cage

The "iron cage" is the product of modern capitalist societies based on rational forms of social organization which create specific qualities. Capitalism ushered in large-scale organizations and institutions that encourage (especially in the workplace) specialized tasks, technical competence, impersonality and personal discipline. The key institution of rationalization is the development of national bureaucracies.
Bureaucracy – by subjecting us all to a set of standard, inflexible rules – ultimately gives rise to societal alienation, stifling regulations and dehumanization. This experience is life in the iron cage.

Structural Functionalism – Talcott Parsons

The next generation of sociologists largely divided into those primarily influenced by either Durkheim or Weber. The US sociologist **Talcott Parsons** (1902–79) aimed to synthesize aspects of Weber and Durkheim with his concept of "**analytical realism**". From Weber, Parsons recognized that sociological observation was impossible without concepts, and all concepts are value-relative. From Durkheim, Parsons accepted that social facts tell us what the world is like.

ANALYTICAL REALISM STATES THAT ALTHOUGH IT IS IMPORTANT TO DEVELOP CONCEPTS TO MAKE CONCEPTS, WE NEED TO CHECK OUR OBSERVATIONS AGAINST THE EVIDENCE.

Parsons argued that sociology needs an "action frame of reference": concepts that enable sociologists to research social behaviour, as distinguished from concepts used to research the natural world. It is of utmost importance that sociologists try to understand things as they appear to the individuals and groups they research. The action frame is used in "**structural functionalism**", which sees society and social groups as systems that are bound together by an overarching social structure.

Parsons felt that the objective of sociologists is to identify all the various parts of the social system and then demonstrate the specific functions they fulfil in the system overall. For example, Parsons argued that the small "nuclear family" (an adult couple and their children) which emerged in industrial society reflected the family's changing function in modern society. The purpose of the contemporary family became to socialize children into their roles, such as class and gender.

GO OUTSIDE AND PLAY FOOTBALL, SON. IT'S NOT HEALTHY FOR A BOY TO STAY COOPED UP INDOORS.

Symbolic Interactionism – Herbert Blumer

Structural functionalism retained a dominant position in sociology until the 1970s. However, some sociologists critique functionalism for ignoring **social action**, the ways in which people think and act in relation to social structures. They also critique it for not being able to take into account social change.

In response, the sociologist **Herbert Blumer** (1900–87) developed a theory of "symbolic interactionism". Symbolic interactionism views society as the product of everyday interactions between people seeking to attain shared goals. Society is seen as the result of members constructing a shared reality via these sustained daily interactions.

Blumer encouraged sociological researchers to uncover the numerous subjective meanings groups give to society. By "subjective", Blumer meant that humans are pragmatic actors who must continually modify their behaviour to the actions of other actors. We are able to react to these actions because we interpret them and treat them as symbolic forms. Society is not merely a fixed structure, as argued by functionalists. Instead, it is made up of fluid and flexible networks of interaction. Sociological research therefore requires greater attention to how people interact and how we as individuals gather a sense of self over time.

Urbanization

Blumer and other symbolic interactionists were largely based at the University of Chicago, and the city of Chicago provided the backdrop for their research.

THE CITY HAD UNDERGONE A MASSIVE TRANSFORMATION AS THE POPULATION INCREASED FROM JUST 1,000 IN 1800 TO 1,689,000 AT THE START OF THE 20TH CENTURY.

Herbert Blumer

Sociology as a discipline now advanced to understand not only the causes of urbanization – the shift from rural areas to cities – but also its considerable consequences for society. Sociologists began to explore the process of social change from relatively small-scale societies to huge and complex cities. Such rapid change, noted sociologists, was caused by the rapid process of urban industrialization, which sucked workers from the countryside into the city.

German sociologist **Ferdinand Tönnies** (1855–1936) made a distinction between **community** (*gemeinschaft*) and **society** (*gesellschaft*).

Gemeinschaft describes societies defined by a shared sense of culture, in which group members are bound together by an obligation to the group. *Gemeinschaft* societies are small-scale, characterized by face-to-face relationships and relatively unchanging and simple forms of hierarchy.

IF MY CROPS FAIL, THE WHOLE COMMUNITY SUFFERS, SO WE ALL LOOK AFTER EACH OTHER.

Gesellschaft is modern urban society, which encourages individual self-interest, competitive behaviour and increasingly complex forms of social stratification based on social class, gender and ethnicity.

I DON'T KNOW MY NEIGHBOURS. I'M TOO BUSY WITH WORK AND MY OWN SOCIAL GROUP.

Georg Simmel (1858–1917), another German thinker, analysed the big city. Simmel noted that the development of the industrial city in the 19th century created **individualism**, as it created a capitalist, mechanized society based on the specialization of tasks. Paradoxically, however, such personal freedom made individuals increasingly reliant on on the complementary activity of others. Societal relationships in the city, stated Simmel, are often reduced to financial transactions.

THE MODERN MIND HAS BECOME MORE AND MORE CALCULATING.

Individualism is pervasive in the industrial city. People want to stand out from the flock. The sociologist **Thorstein Veblen** (1857–1929) coined the phrase "**conspicuous consumption**" to describe city dwellers' obsession with buying goods to display their taste and social class. In some cases, people engage in "**invidious consumption**", an attempt to inspire rank envy from others jealous with the buyer's superior spending capacity.

The most systematic attempt to study city life came from a group of sociologists researching Chicago. Known as the Chicago School, they sought to blend the ideas of Tönnies, Durkheim and Simmel into a theory of urban life. Leading members of the Chicago School were Herbert Blumer, **Robert Park** (1864–1944) and **Ernest Burgess** (1886–1966). They depicted the city of Chicago as a "human ecology" of groups competing for habitat and resources.

The Chicago School conceived of the city as a series of concentric circles. Each circle or zone contained a specific group depending on their relative power and influence, with those closest to the centre holding the greatest social and economic influence.

JUST AS PLANT FORMS COMPETE TO INHABIT NATURAL HABITATS, SO DO DIFFERENT ETHNIC AND SOCIAL GROUPS, BUSINESSES AND HOMEOWNERS AIM TO COLONIZE AREAS OF THE URBAN ENVIRONMENT.

Ernest Burgess

THIS ISN'T A GREAT NEIGHBOURHOOD, BUT IT'S ALL I CAN AFFORD.

Microsociology – Erving Goffman

Broadly speaking, sociological research often divides along the lines of those who conduct macrosociology and those who focus on microsociology.

Macrosociology is largely concerned with a high level of aggregation in relation to patterns of social structure, society and social transformation. It often explores national and even global social forces and their impact on social institutions. While important, macrosociology can overlook the role of individuals and small social groups in acting out and creating society.

Microsociology attends to these concerns by focusing on interactions, often face-to-face, between individuals. A master of microsociology, Erving Goffman conducted research in a wide variety of settings, ranging from so-called mental asylums to fieldwork on the Shetland Islands, off the coast of northern Scotland. Goffman was interested in how we present our self-identity in relation to others.

DA WIND WIS FAAN AWA IDA DARKENIN.

Following the symbolic interactionists, Goffman was concerned with what he termed the "**interaction order**": how we act and behave when in the presence of others.

By examining interaction, Goffman provided an explanation for how society works. The interaction order involves the tacit and unspoken rituals and rules of behaviour that members of society engage in during face-to-face situations. For Goffman, the invisible rules that define interaction reveal wider social structures which we, in turn, make real through action.

Impression Management

Echoing Berger's puppet theatre, Goffman gave a "dramaturgical" analysis of social life. Everyday social life is like a theatre, and people routinely become stage actors who play scripted roles they have been socialized into. In any particular theatre of social life we are either actors or audience. As social actors we try to communicate to our audience a particular impression of the self. By deploying scripts, props, costumes, dialogue and gestures, we perform "impression management". Goffman understood the "self" as only becoming "real" through the act of performance and its reception by others in interaction.

Emotional Labour

While the dramaturgical analogy applies to all aspects of social life, it is particularly evident in commercial settings. **Arlie Hochschild**'s (b. 1940) research on flight attendants in the US expands Goffman's analysis by introducing emotions as central to the interaction order. We are living in a society where the display of emotions is important as a sign of individual identity, though this display can be complicated.

Emotional performance is not just the result of biological factors, but is increasingly controlled by employers. Hochschild notes that employees in customer service professions need to develop "emotional labour", a process by which people are expected to manage their feelings in accordance with organizationally defined rules.

Emotional labour involves us aligning private emotions with organizational expectations and involves either "**deep acting**" or "**surface acting**".

Deep acting occurs when a worker draws upon emotions they believe to be authentic to achieve a strong relationship with customers. Surface acting is when someone displays emotions they believe are inauthentic to conform to work rules and norms.

Like a method actor, the individual worker's identity becomes deeply invested in the performance. Nevertheless, drawing on Marx's concept of alienation, Hochschild argues that workers obliged to display inauthentic emotions may eventually develop a sense of self-estrangement or distress. Researching the work experiences of flight attendants, Hochschild notes the difficulties that these people confront when trying to de-personalize customer abuse.

Contemporary Sociology – Michel Foucault

We have thus far described some of the main figures who have defined the discipline. Some of these scholars continue in different ways to influence the many varied strands of sociology, and contemporary sociologists debate which aspects of their work still provide important insights into modern society.

Yet who are the relatively contemporary sociological thinkers, and what aspects of their work are influential? A good place to start is with **Michel Foucault** (1926–84). Foucault did not necessarily consider his work to be sociology. He was far too much of a polymath – versed in philosophy, historiography, medical science, literary criticism and social theory – to be pigeonholed within one discipline.

Social Constructivism

Foucault's work considers the relationship between power, knowledge and "discourse". Like Weber, Foucault challenged the idea that modern developments are the result of benign and enlightened progress. Instead, modern society works by extending power via increasing forms of surveillance.

Power runs through everything and especially in **discourses**: ideas and language embedded in social institutions. How modern social institutions categorize and classify us, Foucault argued, has the power to construct our social identities. As a result, he is seen as a key figure within social constructivism. Social constructivism implies that social reality is a consequence of social processes and practices.

HOW IS THIS DIFFERENT TO EARLIER CONSTRUCTIVIST APPROACHES, LIKE GOFFMAN'S?

I TAKE THIS PERSPECTIVE FURTHER BY SEEING *ALL* ASPECTS OF SOCIAL LIFE AND IDENTITY AS CONSTRUCTED.

Knowledge Is Power

Foucault's constructivism is evident in one of his greatest themes – the relationship between knowledge and surveillance. Foucault's starting point is that the most important thing to study is "knowledge". Knowledge is the key to social power, as the more knowledge you possess about individuals and groups, the more power you have to control them.

Knowledge is supposed to lead to greater human freedom, like democracy and liberty. But Foucault argues that the collection of knowledge often results in the opposite. Knowledge can be dangerous, as it generates new forms of power and greater self-control. Knowledge can limit our liberty.

WHO CREATES, CONTROLS AND IS CONTROLLED BY KNOWLEDGE?

KNOWLEDGE IS POWER AND IT CAN COMMAND OBEDIENCE.

The relationship between knowledge, power and surveillance can be seen in Foucault's analyses of various types of institutions, which he often tracks over a period of centuries. Foucault shows how institutions gradually developed as forms of social control. A particularly important institution, notes Foucault, is the "asylum". Foucault shows that in medieval times "madness" was not necessarily seen as an illness, as it is currently. Instead, the "mad" were often valued members of their communities, appreciated for their hidden forms of wisdom.

With the advent of the Enlightenment in the 18th century and its emphasis on medical scientific knowledge, "insanity" was distinguished as a separate category from "sanity", and in consequence "insane" people were placed in houses of confinement.

THE INSANE WERE SUDDENLY SEEN AS DEVIANT AND THUS TO BE REMOVED FROM THE REST OF "NORMAL" SOCIETY.

Modern society (from the late 19th century onwards) created the asylum, a new form of hospital designed to be more humane, as it treated insanity as an illness that could be cured. To cure mental illness, more objective knowledge of it was required. A new class of specialists, including professional psychiatrists, was created. By gaining knowledge of insanity, the aim was to control it.

Foucault argued that the development of asylums was less a benevolent move with the patient's recovery in mind than part of what he calls the Great Confinement, the removal of social undesirables, such as the poor, prostitutes, the homeless and the "mad", from public sight.

OUT OF MIND, OUT OF SIGHT. OR IS IT THE OTHER WAY AROUND?

Social Categorization

Rather than lead to the patient's cure, the institution of the modern asylum creates ever increasing forms of social control. Foucault argued that the process of labelling and classifying people as "insane" and "mad" has real social effects, as the patients begin to internalize the characteristics of the definition. In order to "cure" mentally ill people humanely, the process of labelling and categorization relies upon more knowledge, especially better data collection on forms of medical treatment. In response, patients are subjected to experimental treatments and controlled physically, chemically and psychologically.

THERE IS NO SUCH THING AS THE MAD AND THE NORMAL. THEY ARE SOCIAL CONSTRUCTS. THEY ARE CONSTRUCTS OF THE DEVELOPMENT OF CIVILIZATION.

The Prison – Discipline and Punishment

The relationship between knowledge, power and surveillance is further developed in Foucault's analysis of the modern prison. Foucault began his analysis with prisons in medieval Europe. Punishment during this period was public and often spectacularly violent as a means to deter the audience from crime. With the creation of the state prison in the 19th century, punishment became less violent and public.

THE PURPOSE OF THE PRISON IS NOW TO HELP REFORM THE PRISONER.

Keeping records and details about each individual prisoner and what motivated them to take up crime became the purpose of the modern prison and gave birth to the science of criminology.

Criminology provides templates for categorization and labelling; it defines what constitutes a criminal versus a normal, law-abiding citizen. The object of reform is to make the criminal normal again.

What is it about the modern prison that keeps the prisoner controlled and obedient? Foucault pointed to the power of surveillance and monitoring, which makes individuals self-regulate their behaviour. He referred to the English philosopher **Jeremy Bentham** (1748–1832) and his concept of the "**panopticon**". The panopticon is the idea that an individual guard could monitor numerous prisoners without the inmates being able to tell if they were being watched.

As long as prisoners thought they were being observed, the logic was that they would behave. In other words, they would self-regulate their behaviour. The panopticon was the all-seeing eye that provided control without necessarily requiring the immediate physical presence of the guard.

Foucault argued that these processes of surveillance and control, first perfected in the institutions of the asylum and the prison, had expanded outwards to dominate practically all aspects of modern society. In this sense, Foucault shared with Max Weber a concern with how the contemporary world is defined by bureaucratic systems and institutions that promote rationalization and dehumanization.

Three strategies of surveillance are particularly apparent: labelling, visibility and data collection. These forms had spread to other institutions to create a **panopticon society**, which has continued to develop in many contemporary societies, with multiple surveillance systems generating many forms of knowledge for different groups of specialist knowledge holders, from doctors, tax officials, businesses and educationalists to big data companies like Facebook, Google and mobile phone companies.

Surveillance Society

David Lyon (b.1948) explores in more depth the expansion of what he terms "surveillance society" in the modern world. Social institutions utilize increasingly complex forms of electronic data collection on individuals, groups and even whole populations. Big data is gathered to monitor and control practically every aspect of our everyday lives, and requires constant collection and updating.

DATA IS REQUIRED TO MONITOR OUR FINANCIAL SITUATIONS, OUR HEALTH, OUR INDIVIDUAL PREFERENCES AS CONSUMERS, OUR WELFARE REQUIREMENTS AND OUR EDUCATIONAL QUALIFICATIONS.

The state is a major collector of big data; it may claim that data is needed to keep the population healthy and safe. However, Lyon notes that such data collection creates a democratic paradox. In order to protect "freedom", states collect data on us which threatens to restrict our civil liberties. Thus, supposedly to prevent crime and terrorism, the state subjects us to surveillance, often without our knowledge.

Other agencies beyond the state are important in surveillance society. Businesses need information on our purchasing choices so that they can sell us more products.

OUR SOCIAL MEDIA OUTPUT, AND EVEN OUR "LIKES" AND "FAVOURITES", ARE MONITORED AND SCRUTINIZED BY BUSINESSES SO THEY CAN TAILOR PRODUCTS TO MATCH OUR CONSUMER PREFERENCES.

Our data is harvested and sold to the relevant agencies. David Lyon notes that there is now a blurring of the lines between government and business in the exchange of data. The police and security services use data purchased from corporations, including mobile phone records and internet searches. As in the panopticon of the 19th-century prison, we experience being surveilled without being directly aware of the observer.

A particularly obvious example of surveillance in our everyday lives is the growth of closed-circuit television (CCTV). We are told that such surveillance reduces crime and protects the public. It discourages theft and vandalism.

Does this official story ring true? Sociologists have conducted research on people whose job it is to monitor CCTV footage. By observing the observers, sociologists discovered that disproportionately few successful prosecutions are made following arrests based on this footage. Rather than being objective and neutral, the direction of the cameras reflects the biases of the operators, with youths, minority ethnic people, drunks and beggars most often targeted. Instead of stopping crime, surveillance merely shifts crime to another place. It obscures the fact that crime is not merely located in specific groups, but occurs across society.

Failed Consumers

The rise of surveillance is seen by sociologists as generating pernicious effects. Zygmunt Bauman looks at the consequences of CCTV in our consumer culture, making a distinction between "successful" and "failed" consumers. Successful consumers are those able to afford luxury goods, while failed consumers cannot. Consumer culture stimulates the aspirations of all social classes, regardless of whether we can all participate equally.

Shoplifting for consumer goods is the result of the societal pressure to obtain goods. But the aim of CCTV surveillance, argues Bauman, is not only to stop shoplifting by failed consumers. It is more concerned with keeping public spaces – such as shopping malls and high streets – purified from these "undesirable elements", poor people, by making them feel unwelome.

Pierre Bourdieu

Another major figure in contemporary sociological thought is Michel Foucault's French compatriot, **Pierre Bourdieu** (1930–2002). You were briefly introduced to Bourdieu at the beginning of this book. His work, we noted, was primarily concerned with exposing the often subtle forms of domination that legitimize social inequality. Bourdieu originally served with the French army in Algeria during the 1950s and 60s. After leaving the army, he stayed in Algeria to conduct research on issues related to social structure and domination within the Berber group in North Africa. This research established Bourdieu as a leading scholar and eventually as the preeminent sociologist of the modern age.

Bourdieu's research agenda made very important contributions to our understanding of social class, providing a complex sociological analysis of social class in contemporary Western societies. He turned his attention particularly to the public (state) educational system, as it is supposed to be **meritocratic**, which means that it rewards natural ability and hard work, rather than wealth. However, Bourdieu's research demonstrated that education is essential to the reproduction of power and privilege for the dominant group. Education is at the very heart of a system that supports and continues social inequalities.

THE POINT OF MY WORK IS TO SHOW THAT CULTURE AND EDUCATION AREN'T SIMPLY HOBBIES OR MINOR INFLUENCES. THEY ARE HUGELY IMPORTANT IN THE AFFIRMATION OF DIFFERENCES BETWEEN GROUPS AND SOCIAL CLASSES AND IN THE REPRODUCTION OF THOSE DIFFERENCES.

Cultural Capital

Education is universal and it is supposedly meritocratic, a myth which modern nations with expansive welfare states perpetuate.

Key to Bourdieu's analysis of education is the concept of "cultural capital", a phrase he coins (no pun intended) to describe non-economic resources. Cultural capital includes knowledge and skills, things that permit social mobility. Just like any other resource, cultural capital is convertible under some conditions into economic forms, including educational qualifications.

Bourdieu outlined three connected types of cultural capital: "embodied", "objectified" and "institutionalized".

Embodied capital is how cultural capital can be acquired and cultivated. Bourdieu likened "embodied capital" to body-building. We work to make it seem an indispensable part of how we are, to make the muscles (the cultural capital) appear as natural features of the self. At the same time, embodied cultural capital occurs mostly through the transmission of norms and values from our parents and from the social group we belong to. We are socialized into gaining cultural capital. Embodied capital involves a process of learning which eventually becomes habituated for the individual. To gain embodied capital we use cultural goods, like literature and art, which can be converted into qualifications.

Objectified capital is physical forms of culture, such as writings and paintings, which can be used to demarcate a higher social status.

Institutionalized capital is the official documentation and accreditation (such as academic qualifications) that allows the individual to use cultural capital in a way to their economic and social advantage.

In all its forms, cultural capital adds up to a resource that contributes to the success of pupils in the educational system and workers in employment. The dominant groups set standards of excellence throughout schools and universities that reflect their own power and interests. Success at exams depends on the student possessing the required amount of cultural capital. Acquiring the cultural capital of the dominant culture at birth gives students from a dominant class an advantage when they take their exams.

The fact that some working-class children succeed despite lacking wealth in cultural capital appears to confirm the meritocratic character of universal education. Cultural capital obscures the inequalities structurally built into educational institutions.

Distinctions and Taste

In another influential work, Bourdieu examined how the middle class deploy their aesthetic tastes to legitimize class differences. Their cultural preferences are used as the basis for passing judgement on lower ranked groups. Through the exercise of taste, the middle class validate their own position of power and prestige while simultaneously framing the tastes of other social groups as inferior, which naturally acts to maintain their subordinate status in the social structure. The act of cultural consumption, according to Bourdieu, is important in maintaining class distinctions. While class was once seen to be defined by what we produce (our jobs) class is increasingly characterized by what we consume.

Taste in classical music, abstract art and modernist literature (what is often termed "high art") are all part of the cultural capital used by the middle class to demarcate their superiority to the working class and their preferences for mass-produced culture (often termed "low art").

Bourdieu noted, however, that practically all forms of culture can be used to create social boundaries. Thus, if you prefer a soya, decaf latte to instant coffee – this too may express social class distinctions. What matters is not any inherent qualities of these cultural products; more important is the social value we assign to these products. Taste refers to your preferences for a broad range of cultural capital, from clothing, furniture, leisure activities, dinner menus, through, even, to a preference for a slim and healthy body gained by jogging and going to an exclusive gym. These forms are used to create distinctions between social groups.

Social Class

The analysis of class – from Karl Marx onwards – has provided a central area of sociological research. For sociologists, class represents the primary structure through which social divisions are created and maintained. Bourdieu's work is highly significant for sociological research on social class in modern society.

Traditional sociological measures of class have positioned people in social classes according to their occupation and employment status. A person's place within a specific social class is principally determined by whether they work in routine or semi-routine occupations employed on a "labour contract", or in professional or managerial occupations employed on a "service contract". Many sociologists have questioned these traditional measures, however, as this metric for class doesn't capture the full range of social and cultural factors in maintaining class hierarchies.

IF WE WERE TO USE BOURDIEU'S CRITERIA FOR CONCEPTUALIZING CLASS, WHAT MIGHT WE DISCOVER ABOUT OUR OWN POSITION IN THE SOCIAL STRUCTURE?

So far you have already been introduced to Bourdieu's different types of cultural capital. However, to fully understand class, Bourdieu argues that we need to add further forms of "capital" to the equation: a person's class is determined by how much cultural, economic and social capital they are able to gain. The more of each of these capital resources a person is able to accrue, the higher the class formation they can attain. Whereas **economic capital** is based on wealth and income, **social capital** is the social networks people are located in.

Bourdieu's three forms of capital give us a model for identifying social class. Applying Bourdieu's model, sociologists have identified seven specific classes in 21st-century Britain. At the top is a wealthy elite, separated from an established middle class, and a class of newly affluent workers. Underneath reside an ageing working class, a "precariat" with low levels of capital and service workers, such as call centre employees.

Class 1

I AM "ELITE". I AM A PUBLIC RELATIONS DIRECTOR. I WENT TO CAMBRIDGE UNIVERSITY. I HAVE A HIGH HOUSEHOLD INCOME, SUBSTANTIAL SAVINGS AND I SCORE HIGHLY IN STOCKS OF "HIGHBROW" CULTURE.

Class 2: Established middle class

Class 3: Technical middle class

Class 4: New affluent workers

Class 5: Traditional working class

Class 6: Emergent service workers

Class 7

I AM A "PRECARIAT". I AM A POSTAL WORKER. I DIDN'T GO TO UNIVERSITY. I HAVE A LOW HOUSEHOLD INCOME, NEGLIGIBLE SAVINGS, AND I RENT. I HAVE LOW STOCKS OF ALL CAPITAL.

Postmodernism

As we've seen in the work of Foucault, **social progress** does not always have benign ends. The cultivation of knowledge, stated Foucault, can erode democratic development and liberty. Rather than delivering a utopia – as Auguste Comte expected – scientific and technological progress has led to the threat of nuclear and environmental destruction. In consequence, our society is characterized by a lack of faith in the idea of progress.

KNOWLEDGE IS THE KEY TO FREEDOM.

THE EXPANSION OF KNOWLEDGE AS A RESULT OF THE ENLIGHTENMENT IS NOT DELIVERING FREEDOM AND DEMOCRACY BUT INCREASING SOCIAL CONTROL AND DOMINATION.

Since the 1970s, some sociologists have questioned the concept of social progress and the legitimacy of sociology in contributing to progress. This anxiety is often seen as indicative of "postmodernism": the idea that there has been a disruptive break with modernity and its emphasis on progress.

Metanarratives

The postmodern rupture with progress is caused by a widespread lack of faith in science and technology and in political and social transformation. **Jean-François Lyotard** (1924–98) defined the "postmodern condition" as symptomized by the end of "metanarratives".

Metanarratives are claims and theories that are totalizing and universalizing. They are master stories that explain history and society as possessing a universal truth.

One metanarrative is the idea that history is driven by an internal logic to reach some universal end point. The Marxist claim that historical progress will lead to global communism is a metanarrative. As is the idea that free-market democracy is an inevitable end point of history.

Jean-François Lyotard

HISTORICAL PROGRESS WILL LEAD TO GLOBAL COMMUNISM!

MARX, I'M TIRED OF THIS METANARRATIVE.

Lyotard argued that there is incredulity to metanarratives in our society. We are wary of any political ideology or scientific claim that speaks about progress. We fear metanarratives because they are homogenizing and silencing. They act to exclude and even violently expel individuals, groups and ways of life that do not fit into them. We are, furthermore, deeply sceptical about the role of science and technology in the modern world.

KNOWLEDGE IS NO LONGER ABOUT HUMAN FREEDOM BUT THE EXERCISE OF POWER.

Knowledge, in the form of information, is used by governments as a tool of social control rather than as a device to eradicate social problems. Lyotard claimed that knowledge is produced and used via two forms – the **field** and **legitimation**. The field reveals that those with the ability to collect data and knowledge control its meaning. Legitimation is how knowledge is determined by the intersecting forces of power, authority and government.

Postmodernism has implications for sociology, a discipline which was borne of modernity and a desire to understand social change. As we've seen, many sociologists argue that social theory and analysis is not just a means to describe society.

For Auguste Comte, the science of sociology is to predict the future course of society by uncovering the laws or principles that govern history. This is **Historicism** – the idea that there are historical laws of social development. History has a necessary direction and end point. The ultimate goal of sociology is social engineering, helping to reform and improve society through progress.

Postmodernism questions sociology's claim to be a social science concerned with progress and reform. The postmodernist perspective claims that we can never possess enough knowledge of society to identify laws and that human knowledge changes over time anyway. Nor can sociologists ever fully remove individual political and cultural biases from their research. Postmodernists, finally, question the deployment of positivism, the bedrock of the discipline's methodology.

ONCE I'VE FINISHED COLLECTING DATA, I'LL KNOW EVERYTHING AND WILL BE ABLE TO MAKE POSITIVE CHANGES TO SOCIETY.

NO YOU WON'T. YOUR DATA IS COMPROMISED BY YOUR PERSONAL BIASES. PLUS, YOU CAN NEVER *KNOW* SOCIETY; IT'S IMPOSSIBLE.

Sociology and Gender

Rather conspicuous absences in this book so far are the voices of female sociologists and the sociological analysis of gender. This gender gap reveals that the formation and early development of the discipline were largely dominated by men. Since the object of sociology is to challenge socially produced inequalities and divisions, it is noteworthy that women and gender were not always at the heart of the discipline. The situation is now very different, as since the 1970s the analysis of gender has become one of the leading contributions of sociology. Women, moreover, are leaders of the discipline, not just in the area of gender but across a range of sociology fields.

Biological or Socially Constructed?

Are differences between men and women a result of our nature, our genes, or the society we live in? Sociologists argue that gender differences are socially constructed: that our gender identities are not merely the result of biological sexual differences, but that we *become* gendered and actively reproduce our gender roles.

Sociologists refute **biological determinism**, the **essentialist** idea that gender inequalities are caused by innate biological characteristics, such as differences in hormones and anatomy. Applying essentialism often legitimizes structural inequalities between men and women.

WOMEN SHOULD BE NURSES, CHILDMINDERS AND TEACHERS, AS THESE JOBS REFLECT THEIR NATURAL CARING EMOTIONS.

ISN'T IT FUNNY HOW THESE JOBS ARE PAID WORSE THAN SUPPOSEDLY "MALE JOBS", LIKE BUSINESS MANAGERS? WE NEED TO STOP SAYING THAT WOMEN'S JOB CHOICE SHOULD BE RESTRICTED BASED ON THEIR SUPPOSED NATURAL CAPACITIES.

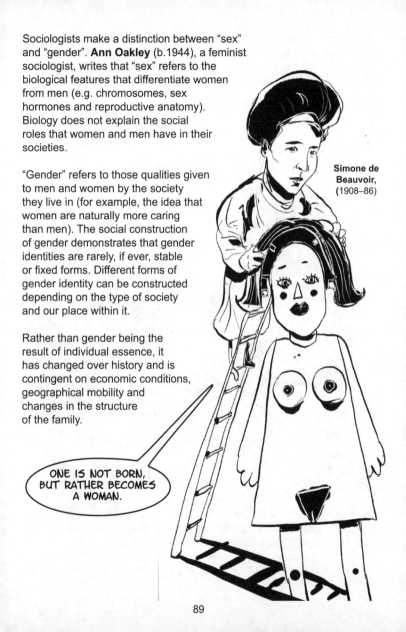

Sociologists make a distinction between "sex" and "gender". **Ann Oakley** (b.1944), a feminist sociologist, writes that "sex" refers to the biological features that differentiate women from men (e.g. chromosomes, sex hormones and reproductive anatomy). Biology does not explain the social roles that women and men have in their societies.

"Gender" refers to those qualities given to men and women by the society they live in (for example, the idea that women are naturally more caring than men). The social construction of gender demonstrates that gender identities are rarely, if ever, stable or fixed forms. Different forms of gender identity can be constructed depending on the type of society and our place within it.

Rather than gender being the result of individual essence, it has changed over history and is contingent on economic conditions, geographical mobility and changes in the structure of the family.

Simone de Beauvoir, (1908–86)

ONE IS NOT BORN, BUT RATHER BECOMES A WOMAN.

The social construction of gender, sociologists argue, occurs at all stages of our lives, starting from the moment we're assigned one of two sexes at birth. We are subsequently socialized into thinking that our gender identities are normal and just the way things are. Talcott Parsons argued that socialization leads to us accepting specific gender roles, with women adopting specifically feminine attributes and men adopting masculine attributes.

A "PROPER" WOMAN IS EXPRESSIVE, EMOTIONAL AND SENSITIVE. SHE CARES FOR THE FAMILY.

MEN ARE INSTRUMENTAL, RATIONAL AND COMPETITIVE. WE PROVIDE FOR AND PROTECT OUR FAMILIES.

We quickly internalize the appropriate gender roles given to us and transmit them from generation to generation. Individuals who fail to conform to their given gender roles are labelled as societal "deviants". The consequences of such labelling can range from gossip to communal ostracism and violence.

Parsons was a structural functionalist, which means that he viewed gender as a set of roles that play a part in the overall functioning of a stable society. He didn't argue that gender roles in society are a good thing; however, he identified that the exercise of gender divisions is crucial in maintaining societal equilibrium. Gender divisions undergirded the division of labour, segmenting the sphere of employment on gender lines, with different forms of employment traditionally reserved for men and women.

Gender Performance

In contrast to structural functionalism, in the constructivist perspective, gender is not merely a role we are given through socialization, in which we as individuals have little or no part. Instead, social constructivists point to how we can actively reshape our gender identity and even *perform* gender. There are many ways of being a man or a woman, which are often situational in relation to other social factors, such as class and ethnicity.

We have already seen the sociological idea that we perform and act out our social roles in interaction with others. Erving Goffman called this the "interaction order". Our sense of self only becomes "real" when it is performed and when others accept the validity of this act. Goffman argued that social practices do not "express" natural gender differences so much as produce them. What we understand to be "biological" markers of sex – such as genitalia – are insignificant prior to social interaction and the rich forms of meaning we give to them as indicators of social distinction.

OUR GENDERED IDENTITIES ARE MANAGED PRESENTATIONS RATHER THAN EXPRESSIONS OF INTERNAL TRUTHS.

Our sense of gender arises through routinized and managed interaction with others within shared communities of understanding about what gender "is" and what it "means".

The performance metaphor is expanded by the radical feminist scholar **Judith Butler** (b.1956). Gender has a script, and it has been rehearsed through our socialization process, but we are the main actors who perform gender by how we dress, walk, talk and consume culture. Butler celebrates the drag queen – a character, usually male, who performs a rather exaggerated and stereotypical vision of femininity. For Butler, the drag queen exposes the performative elements of all gender identities.

However, because we do not ordinarily see gender as performative, we fail to see how existing definitions of gender in our society reproduce inequalities between men and women. The task of sociologists at the outset is to challenge essentialist notions of gender. By unmasking the constructed and performative role of gender, we can start to deal with the structure of disadvantage experienced by women in society. The rules underlying gender are historically grounded and rely on their continual enactment by subjects. Butler draws our attention to any performance of gender that questions what is real and authentic.

THE TRANSVESTITE'S GENDER IS AS REAL AS ANYONE WHOSE PERFORMANCE COMPLIES WITH SOCIAL EXPECTATIONS. IF THE "REALITY" OF GENDER IS CONSTITUTED BY THE PERFORMANCE, THEN THERE IS NO ESSENTIAL AND UNREALIZED "SEX" OR "GENDER" WHICH GENDER PERFORMANCES EXPRESS.

Judith Butler

The Gender Order

All societies around the world are defined by gender divisions, arranged so that wealth, power and privilege are unequally distributed between men and women. Gender is not just about the construction of social differences, it is also an identity that justifies inequalities, exploitation and the domination of men over women, a form of social organization known as **patriarchy**.

A key issue for sociologists researching gender is to demonstrate the specific ways in which patriarchy operates. Patriarchy may reveal itself in rather obvious ways, such as the assumption that men should automatically be the breadwinners of the household and women the homemakers. However, the situation is more complex.

DO THE SIMPLE ACTS OF WOMEN WEARING MAKE-UP OR DIETING REPRODUCE GENDER DIFFERENCES AND WOMEN'S SUBORDINATE SOCIAL POSITION?

DOES THE INSTITUTION OF MARRIAGE, OR HAVING CHILDREN, PERPETUATE INEQUALITIES?

Hegemonic Masculinity

To fully understand the operation of patriarchy, it is also necessary to analyse how men maintain their position of power in society. Sociologists attend to the way in which masculinity is constructed within a particular society. The Australian sociologist **R.W. Connell** (b.1944) developed the term "hegemonic masculinity" to describe the construction of particular forms of male identity that support patriarchy. Hegemonic masculinity is a culturally idealized form of masculine character that maintains a structure of dominance and oppression in the gender order. It provides a template against which all men in that society position themselves.

Connell argues that the role of the sociologist is to identify the various forms of hegemonic masculinity and to reveal how it underpins the very structure of social organization.

Patriarchy and hegemonic masculinity may legitimate gender inequalities, but the system does not benefit all men equally. Some men are more advantaged than others by hegemonic masculinity. These men construct a sense of masculinity that contributes to their overall resources in social, economic and cultural capital. Men in higher social classes, or of the ethnic majority, are able to benefit more from patriarchy than those from a lower social class, or an ethnic minority. In the same building, a white, middle-class office manager will enjoy greater privileges than an ethnic minority, migrant cleaner.

DIFFERENT CONCEPTIONS OF HEGEMONIC MASCULINITY CAN BE FOUND DEPENDING ON THE SOCIAL CLASS. THE RULES OF HEGEMONIC MASCULINITY ALSO VARY ACROSS SOCIAL GROUPS.

Masculinity in Transformation

The broad changes in the late 20th and early 21st centuries affecting the traditional role of women and families in industrial society has raised important questions about masculinity and its changing role in society.

In Western societies, it is also often the case that more women than men attend university. Rather than a clear division of labour along gender lines, men and women compete for the same jobs. This situation has forced men to cultivate and take care of their bodies and appearance, and to use their emotional labour in ways that were once expected of women in the workplace. Women have successfully overturned the norm that men are the main earners and leaders of the family.

Masculinity in Crisis

Connell argues that hegemonic masculinity is an ideal identity, which very few men can reasonably live up to. Those able to harness it gain a superior position in society, benefitting from what Connell calls the "patriarchal dividend".

What about men unable to convincingly live up to the ideal? It is claimed that there is a "crisis of masculinity" as traditionally male roles have come under threat. Some sociologists argue that men in Western societies are more likely to suffer from depression and even have suicidal feelings from the loss of their status.

WE CONFRONT A WORK ENVIRONMENT CHARACTERIZED BY CHANGING JOB ROLES, THE THREAT OF REDUNDANCY AND DOWNSIZING.

I FACE PRESSURE TO LIVE UP TO OLD-FASHIONED MACHISMO, AS WELL AS NURTURING A "NEW MAN" IDENTITY.

Homosexual Masculinity

Connell argues that there are a number of subordinate masculinities and femininities arranged hierarchically underneath the hegemonic masculinity. Among these subordinate forms is homosexual masculinity. If hegemonic masculinity is seen as the embodiment of manhood, then in our gender-ordered society, the gay man is seen as the opposite. Connell is not claiming that gay men are inferior, but he understands that homosexuality is a stigmatized identity and ranks at the bottom of the gender hierarchy for men.

HEGEMONIC MASCULINITY SUPPORTS A FORM OF HETEROSEXUAL IDENTITY THAT LEGITIMATES AND IS SUSTAINED BY HOMOPHOBIA, HATRED FOR GAY MEN, WHO ARE SEEN AS THE OPPOSITE OF "NORMAL" MALE IDENTITY.

Race and Ethnicity

The sociological study of race and ethnicity is almost as old as the discipline itself. A major reason for this is the contribution of **W.E.B. Du Bois** (1868–1963), an African-American sociologist, major social reformer and civil rights activist. Du Bois studied sociology at Harvard and was the first African American to receive a PhD there. Through his work on the social worlds of African-American populations, Du Bois made a valuable contribution both to the study of race and discrimination, and to the use of statistics and graphs in sociological research. In a study of an African-American district of Philadelphia, Du Bois drew on interviews, personal observations and documents to record the lives of the black community.

Du Bois's early research was on African-American "slum" communities in the US city of Philadelphia. By studying these communities as a social system, Du Bois was the first sociologist to systematically explore how racism functioned as part of the social and economic structure.

Racism is not just a philosophical perspective that black people are inferior to white people. The object of prejudice and discrimination against black people is to create a cheap pool of labour for capitalists to exploit.

In *Black Reconstruction in America 1860–1880* (1935), Du Bois applied a Marxist analysis to race.

> EMANCIPATION OF MAN IS THE EMANCIPATION OF LABOUR, AND THE EMANCIPATION OF LABOUR IS THE FREEING OF THAT BASIC MAJORITY OF WORKERS WHO ARE YELLOW, BROWN AND BLACK.

In his early writings, Du Bois hoped that benevolent white leaders and business people could be harnessed to bring about social reform and the end of racism. Eventually he concluded that these people had no reason to resolve the race question as they prospered from a racially divided society.

Double Consciousness

Du Bois was particularly interested in how African Americans experience and understand racism in their daily lives. He coined the term "double consciousness" to describe how black people internalize discrimination and prejudice, caught in the cross-pressures of an American system which prides itself on equality and fairness while simultaneously practising racial discrimination. The culture of black society and the psychology of individual members is often based on looking at themselves through the eyes of racist, white America. The double consciousness arises as a result of black people trying to integrate into American society while maintaining a distinct racial identity.

Sociology and Migration

One of the key areas of sociological research into race and ethnicity is migration. The USA has famously been described as a country built by migrants, and many counties in Western Europe have been transformed since the end of WWII into migrant societies. While migration can be involuntary – such as refugees fleeing war zones – sociologists often explore the complex factors involved in *voluntary* migration, such as dissatisfaction with living conditions in the home country and hope for a better life in wealthier regions. In many cases, states have pulled in migrants to address labour shortages. Estimates suggest that there are more than 220 million migrants across the globe.

Sociologists examine the various forms in which racism is applied to migrants in post-war Europe. They look at "**racialization**", the process by which society is divided up into groups that are supposed to possess essential racial features, such as skin colour and language. Sociologists argue that racialization is often used to define particular minority groups as inferior in order to justify discrimination and to legitimize the power of the majority group over them.

"**Racism**" is a term used by sociologists to describe those institutions and social processes of disadvantage and inequality that are built around a discourse of racial discrimination. "**Institutional racism**" describes public institutions that systematically disadvantage minority groups. For example, the police services in the UK and the USA have been accused of operating institutional racism due to their treatment of minority ethnic populations.

Cultural Racism

Sociologists studying migration and race note that the language used to legitimate racism shifted from the 1960s onwards. While the language of racism once emphasized a perceived mental and intellectual superiority of whites over non-whites, cultural identity is now used to justify racism. The sociologist **Paul Gilroy** (b.1956) showed how Afro-Caribbean settlers in the UK were being framed by the media and politicians as having cultural values that were simply incompatible with Britishness. Afro-Caribbean males were portrayed as "pimps" in the 1950s and as "muggers" in the 1980s.

THE FOCUS ON "BLACK CRIME" IS A DEVICE TO MAKE MIGRANTS APPEAR AS A THREAT TO NATIONAL COHESION AND SECURITY. CRIME IS "RACIALIZED" AND GENDERED.

The new cultural racism is linked to the political transformation of Britain at the end of the 1970s. Gilroy argued that Britain had entered a long-term economic and political crisis as it simultaneously lost its empire and its manufacturing base. In this context, the politics of race and nation created a new culturally-focused racism. Representations of migrants stressed their alienness and the supposed criminal inclinations of the black population. Key areas of state intervention in schooling and policing were shown by Gilroy and other sociologists to be informed by cultural racism.

MIGRANTS PROVIDED A CONVENIENT SCAPEGOAT FOR BRITAIN'S POST-WAR ECONOMIC DECLINE.

THINGS HAVE BEEN WORSE ROUND HERE SINCE THEY SHOWED UP.

THEY'RE NOT LIKE US.

The power of cultural racism is that it can be applied across a range of countries to their migrants. In cultural racism, the host nation constructs itself as an ethnically homogenous national society whose traditional ways of life are threatened by migrants who supposedly refuse to integrate. The cultural identities of migrants are therefore seen as a threat to national harmony and as incompatible with the host society. Cultural racism is based on a form of **xenophobia**, a deep fear of people with different cultural identities. Alongside a perceived cultural threat, migrants may be constructed as threats to national cohesion, by being accused of taking away jobs from members of the host nation.

Islamophobia

Patterns of migration have changed over the decades in Britain and in many other European states as new groups of settlers arrive. Does cultural racism shift to reflect the relationship between the host country and the new migrant population? One way to address this question, sociologists claim, is by looking at the emergence of Islamophobia in some Western countries. Islamophobia centres on a fear that the identities and cultural practices of Muslim migrants supposedly represent a threat to core Western values, such as human rights, democracy and the separation of religion and state.

Sociologists have explored how the issue of women's rights is used to justify the discourse of Islamophobia. For example, some Western newspapers concentrate on the practice of female genital mutilation (FGM) by some Muslim groups originally from sub-Saharan Africa, which is framed as harming women's rights. The wearing of the hijab or the burka by some Muslim women is also made out to be in opposition to Western values that allow freedom of choice for individuals. Sociologists argue that the object of Islamophobia is to present Muslim migrants as dangerous presences within so-called "progressive" and "democratic" Western states.

Multiculturalism

The use of culture to describe the perceived differences of migrant groups is examined by sociologists in relation to public policies. A particularly important example of this is the policy of multiculturalism. Multiculturalism is based on the idea that minority ethnic groups have cultural identities distinct from the host population. These cultural identities ought to be recognized and accommodated by the host state.

Multiculturalism can be seen as in opposition to the assimilationist policy of trying to make migrants conform to the values and norms of the host society.

Where does the idea of multiculturalism come from? In fact, it developed as a system to end racism and discrimination. A key thinker in developing the idea is the German-American anthropologist **Franz Boas** (1858–1942).

Boas's writings occurred in the context of, and in opposition to, scientific racism, a body of research which claimed that there were clear physical and biological traits that hierarchically distinguished races. Science provided a cloak of academic respectability for justifying racial discrimination since white Europeans were placed at the head of the hierarchy with other races arranged below.

Cultural Relativism

Boas argued that there are no fundamental racial differences between humans. Instead, culture is more important in defining variations in human civilization. The cultural communities – ethnic, religious and national – that we are born into, Boas claimed, shape who we are as humans and how we relate to our society.

Standards and values are relative to the culture from which they come. For this reason, Boas stated that it is impossible to compare and rank cultures. The premise that all cultures *cannot* be ranked hierarchically is "cultural relativism". Cultural relativists state we should not only celebrate cultural diversity, but accept it as key part of how society is made up.

Recognition

Multiculturalists argue that because humans associate as members of groups bound together by shared cultural identities, they desire to have their identities recognized by other groups. When other groups refuse to recognize, or they demean, another group's cultural identities, this causes oppression and injustice.

Multiculturalism requires that we recognize the particular cultural identities of minority ethnic groups, as this contributes to a more tolerant society. These cultural identities include religious practices, language, music and art. State multiculturalism accommodates faith-based schools, and the cultural identities of minority ethnic groups are included in school curricula, public media and even affirmative action (positive discrimination) in terms of public housing and job allocation.

Multiculturalism represents an alternative to traditional concepts of societal equality.

The individual-integrationist approach assumes that we are all individuals and, as a consequence, the state should not make any distinction between us. Sociologist **Tariq Modood** (b. 1952) suggests that the multicultural accommodation of minorities is different from integration because it explicitly recognizes the social reality of groups. We cannot simply wish away the cultural identities of migrant groups.

Individual-integrationist approach to ethnic diversity

EQUALITY AND JUSTICE MEANS TREATING EVERYBODY THE SAME.

I AM NOT JUST AN INDIVIDUAL. MY GROUP HAS DIFFERENT VALUES AND NEEDS. WE CAN'T BE TREATED EXACTLY THE SAME AS OTHER GROUPS.

Multicultural approach

While assimilation requires migrant groups to adapt their cultural practices to fit with the host population, multiculturalism should be one of mutual adjustment.

The goal of multiculturalism is to spread understanding between the host population and migrants so that they can eventually build a shared sense of understanding and national identity.

Critiquing Multiculturalism

Do all sociologists agree that multiculturalism supports progressive anti-racist politics? Many sociologists worry that multiculturalism may actually produce the opposite. **Kenan Malik** (b. 1960) argues that multiculturalism encourages people to think of themselves as belonging to separate groups and it legitimates the ghettoization of society, where these separate groups do not interact with one another.

Kenan Malik

Bauman argues that multiculturalism restricts the possibility of groups in society coming together to overcome various forms of inequality and discrimination. Since multiculturalism legitimates the idea of separateness between groups, it makes it all the more difficult for a serious cross-cultural dialogue to take place.

Essentialism vs Interculturalism

Multiculturalism is also critiqued for freezing culture and group identities in time: promoting essentialism in which ethnic groups are assumed to be homogeneous and timeless entities. In contrast to multiculturalism's supposed essentialism, some sociologists instead encourage an "interculturalist" approach to society.

The interculturalist approach accepts that there are no such things as pure cultures, which belong simply to one group or another. In the interculturalist viewpoint, we should encourage cultural mixing and **hybridity** – the blending together of various cultural forms to create something new which represents the best of all the groups living in society.

Globalization

THE LIFE OF THE INDIVIDUAL ANYWHERE IS AFFECTED BY EVENTS AND PROCESSES EVERYWHERE.

We are living in a world of increasing interconnectedness. Local events and areas are influenced by processes that take place on a global scale. They may be stimulated by global warming and climate change or by the expansion of financial markets and multinational corporations. As a result, people are developing a consciousness of the world as one place. This process is called globalization. The impact of globalization on our social worlds has become a major sociological theme, though sociologists rarely agree on either the underlying causes of globalization or its main consequences.

Time–Space Compression

Our world appears to be shrinking and our lives are experienced at a frenetic pace due to speedier means of transport and communication. The sociologist and geographer **David Harvey** (b.1935) describes this compression of geographic space as "time–space compression".

For example, in the 18th century the average speed of wind-powered sail boats (the primary mode of long-distance travel) was 10 miles per hour; in the 21st century jet-engine aircrafts can propel us across the globe at 500 miles per hour. Digital means of communication – such as the internet and satellite technology – reduce the gap between absolute and relative distance (the miles between places vs the distance based on prevailing technology).

Time–space compression, then, is driven by scientific and technological advancements. Harvey complicates this clear line of causality by arguing that such developments are themselves produced by recent shifts in capitalist commodity production.

TECHNOLOGICAL CHANGES HAVE COME ABOUT BOTH TO SPEED UP THE GLOBAL FLOWS OF CAPITAL AND COMMODITIES AND TO ALLOW FOR NEW MARKETS TO BE OPENED AND EXPANDED INTERNATIONALLY.

need to speed up global flows of capital

↓

desire to open up & expand markets

↓

technological & scientific advancements

↓

time–space compression

Time–Space Distanciation

Is the experience of compression the same over space and regardless of people's different degrees of access to fast travel? If our world is shrinking, what impact does this have for social relationships? The British sociologist **Anthony Giddens** (b.1938) uses the phrase "time–space distanciation" to address these questions. In traditional societies, social interaction needs co-presence or face-to-face relationships. Co-presence makes the here and now extremely important. Giddens argues that globalization has intensified the capacity of people who are far apart and in different time zones to communicate and interact.

SOCIAL SYSTEMS ARE NEVER COMPLETELY CUT OFF FROM EACH OTHER IN GLOBALIZATION BUT ARE OFTEN CONNECTED IN A NETWORK.

Anthony Giddens

World-System Theory

Immanuel Wallerstein (b.1930) agrees that globalization is the outcome of the development of capitalism. He calls capitalism a "world-system" that has matured in the late 20th century after centuries of development.

A WORLD-SYSTEM MEANS THAT THERE IS AN OVERARCHING ECONOMIC SYSTEM AT WORK TODAY THAT ENABLES SOME STATES TO ECONOMICALLY AND POLITICALLY EXPLOIT OTHER STATES.

Immanuel Wallerstein

Starting in the 16th century, technological advancement and market institutions stimulated Europeans to explore other parts of the globe for resources and trade, especially for natural resources. This nourished capitalist development, which Wallerstein describes as the "endless accumulation of capital", and which brings with it a constant search to find cheaper raw materials and new consumers.

Core and Periphery

The world-system means that no state can remain completely outside the capitalist framework. All states, whether or not they want to be, are connected and integrated into the system. The question is: where does each country stand within the overall system? Wallerstein introduces a "core–periphery" relationship between states in the system.

Core states are economically and militarily powerful and are in the vanguard leading technological development. They use their power to exploit the poorer and weaker **peripheral states** by extracting their raw materials (such as oil, gas and minerals) and cheap labour. Peripheral nations are often politically unstable and workers experience bad working conditions. As they typically owe vast financial debts to the core, they end up reliant on aid from the core. Acting as a buffer are s**emi-peripheral states**, places that are industrializing and have enough power to stop the core from exploiting them.

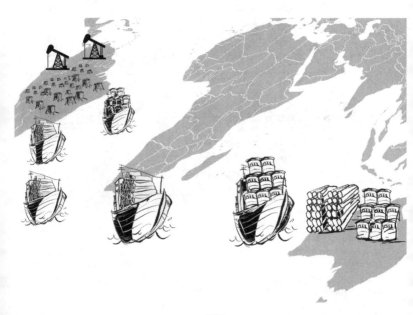

World-system theory makes us think about the world as one big place. To understand any country sociologically, it is necessary to see this country's position in the world-system as either members of the core, semi-periphery or periphery.

Wallerstein does not argue that the capitalist world-system is set in stone. Over time, some countries may experience a change in position or become particularly powerful leaders of the system.

Cultural Globalization

Time–space compression and world-systems are Marxist theories of globalization. They are Marxist theories as they emphasize that globalization is the product of capitalist development and that it creates a world defined by ever widening socioeconomic inequalities. There are also non-Marxist sociological theories of globalization. A key debate between Marxist and non-Marxist sociologists is whether globalization is creating cultural homogeneity (sameness) or cultural heterogeneity (difference), both of which we'll explore in more detail in the next pages.

Homogeneity

Marxist theories often emphasize that globalization spawns cultural homogeneity, with identikit cultural commodities mass-produced by core countries being consumed across the globe. Cultural homogenization destroys local practices and cultures by supplanting them with practices and cultures from the core states.

When cultural homogenization is used to maintain unequal economic relations between core and periphery, it can be read as evidence of cultural imperialism. The USA, in particular, uses its economic power to ensure the domination of US consumer brands (and vice versa) like Apple, Coca-Cola, Starbucks and McDonalds. The same could be said about the supremacy of US mass-media companies, like CNN, Disney and Warner. This reflects the USA's position as the leader of the core countries.

THE APPEARANCE OF THE SAME CONSUMER GOODS EVERYWHERE AROUND THE GLOBE CREATES THE SAME WAYS OF THINKING EVERYWHERE.

A sophisticated example of the homogenization thesis is **Georg Ritzer**'s (b.1940) analysis of "McDonaldization", which draws on Max Weber's idea of formal rationality. Weber contended that modern societies are characterized by an increasing tendency towards the predominance of formally rational systems.

Georg Ritzer

Ritzer argues that the principles of the McDonald's approach to fast-food restaurants (that is, its rational system) are coming to dominate other sectors of American society and of other societies throughout the world.

The main features of McDonaldization are efficiency, calculability, predictability and control, particularly through the substitution of non-human for human technology. McDonaldization is to take a task and then break it down to the smallest level. These tasks are then rationalized to find the most efficient, logical sequence of methods that can be completed the same way every time to produce the desired, predictable outcome. Additionally, quantity (or calculability) becomes the measurement of good performance.

Ritzer argues that these principles have been exported from fast food into almost all institutions across the globe. Because of this, it can be seen as an example of global homogenization.

Heterogeneity

One major criticism of the claim that globalization creates sameness concerns culture. Although sociologists accept that cultural processes have become global, these cultural flows paint a complex picture. Exposure to culture does not necessarily lead to ideological conversion.

Groups across the world consume the same cultural forms, but they adapt them or change their meanings to make them resonate with their local customs and experiences. In one sense, this can happen when global companies alter their products for local conditions. Thus, Starbucks in India provides specific flavours for the local market.

Heterogeneity also occurs when local populations reinterpret or adapt global cultural commodities to reflect their particular experiences. **Ien Ang** (b. 1954) looked at how viewers around the world watched the 1980s US soap opera, *Dallas*. Ang noted that these viewers in different countries interpreted the TV show in very different ways.

Glocalization

This meeting point between local tradition and global modernity is seen by some sociologists as evidence of hybridity, the idea that two or more different forms can be put together to make something new. **Roland Robertson** (b.1938) coined the term "glocalization" to explain how people always reinterpret global cultural products in light of their own local culture. Global culture has to be understood as limited by its reception in local cultures.

Roland Robertson

GLOCALIZATION IS THE SUM OF THE MIX OF GLOBAL AND LOCAL CULTURES.

Glocalization also stems from the marketing strategies of multinational companies, who, to sell their products across the globe, tailor both their advertisements and the products themselves to suit the cultural identities of local groups.

Risk Society

If globalization is so intensive, then it surely must profoundly transform our societies? The German sociologist **Ulrich Beck** (1944–2015) thought so. He argued that globalization has unleashed forces it cannot fully control, producing what Beck called a "risk society". Risk, here, is a contemporary social condition in which man-made dangers create feelings of uncertainty. Beck outlined a number of important aspects that contribute to "risk".

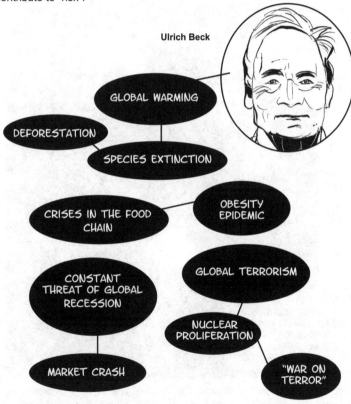

Ulrich Beck

GLOBAL WARMING

DEFORESTATION

SPECIES EXTINCTION

CRISES IN THE FOOD CHAIN

OBESITY EPIDEMIC

CONSTANT THREAT OF GLOBAL RECESSION

GLOBAL TERRORISM

NUCLEAR PROLIFERATION

MARKET CRASH

"WAR ON TERROR"

Beck argued that risks are global in scope and go well beyond national borders. We, in our daily lives, must deal with multiple risks. Our governments and public institutions are poorly equipped to deal with risks, which exacerbates the sense of constant crisis and uncertainty. Beck traced our current attitudes and systems back, outlining how society has changed over the centuries in response to risk. In the late medieval period, risks and hazards were mostly naturally occurring, such as earthquakes, volcanic eruptions and plagues.

IN THE LATE MEDIEVAL PERIOD, HUMANS REACTED TO RISKS AS PRODUCTS OF THE NATURAL WORLD, FATE OR AS ACTS OF GOD.

This age was overtaken by what Beck called "first modernity", a period stretching from the 17th century to the 1960s. This period developed through the intensification of economic, political, cultural and social modernization.

First Modernity

First modernity was characterized by the emergence of an industrial factory-based economy that uses natural raw materials to mass-produce goods. These societies believe that there are unlimited natural resources to be used as they wish. Modernization also creates new political developments: citizens' rights develop alongside the growth of democratic governments. Eventually populations demand social rights, like public housing, employment and healthcare. This leads to the formation of a welfare state. In consequence, the state becomes more powerful as it intervenes in more areas of public life.

First modernity also enables a radical transformation of social life. We witness a process of de-traditionalization. Old forms of hierarchy and custom are less apparent, such as religious authority.

Second Modernity

Second modernity – risk society – unleashes the forces of "**reflexive modernization**". Although Beck is not specific about when second modernity starts, it generally coincides with the 1970s and the end of the **post-war consensus**, the belief that a mixed economy and a strong welfare state produces a fair society. Risk society also reflects our society's awareness of the growing threat of global issues, such as financial markets and the environment.

138

In second modernity, our sense of risk comes from "man-made" problems, even ironically from social policies that are supposed to benefit us. While full employment and the welfare state once provided a safety net for individuals, this has all but disappeared in second modernity. People now often work on short-term contracts, fear downsizing and thus have little job security. In second modernity, science and technology are no longer seen as benign and leading to human progress. Instead we distrust science and are fearful of its consequences for the world.

Reacting to Risk

How do we, as societies and individuals, respond to the risk society of second modernity? Some sociologists are interested in the various ways that we try to offset risk and regain a sense of security and control over our lives. Sociologists admit that this is not easy, and such attempts can have rather problematic outcomes.

Risk society may encourage us to become individuals, but this also leaves us rootless and isolated. In response, we can try to forge a sense of community to give us belonging and security. But at the worst, this can lead to the construction of xenophobic and even racist forms of community.

New Opportunities?

Ulrich Beck believed that globalism and risk society open up new opportunities for positive social change. If many of the problems we confront are of a global nature, then this requires us to adopt a global mindset to deal with them. These global problems include climate change, environmental destruction, food risks, nuclear weapons, global financial risks, genetic cloning and the "war on terror". Beck pointed out that the nation-state no longer has the individual power to successfully address these problems.

Beck believed that the political and economic power of many nation-states is beginning to dwindle, and that this is not wholly a bad thing. Beck saw an opportunity for us to begin dealing with global problems by cooperating across borders.

POLITICAL AND ECONOMIC DECISIONS ARE NOW LARGELY DEVOLVED TO INSTITUTIONS BEYOND THE STATE: THE EU, WORLD BANK, NATO, UNITED NATIONS AND THE INTERNATIONAL MONETARY FUND.

The Cosmopolitan Vision

Beck implored us to develop a "cosmopolitan vision". Instead of only thinking about our individual national interests and concerns, we should see how our collective futures and fates are bound together on a global scale. Beck realized that nation-states are becoming powerless, but he didn't believe that multinational institutions and corporations have a cosmopolitan imagination. Beck saw ordinary people as the key actors in this process.

WE MUST ORGANIZE AT A GRASSROOTS LEVEL TO GENERATE A POLITICS THAT CAN EFFECT CHANGE ACROSS THE GLOBE.

Global Civil Society

The cosmopolitan vision is evident in the development of global civil society: the sphere of ideas, values, institutions, organizations, networks and individuals which operate beyond the confines of families, national societies, polities and economies. Global civil society is seen as evidence of "globalization from below".

Instead of allowing globalization to be shaped top-down by multinational corporations, global civil society is the attempt by ordinary citizens to take control of the process. For example, people power can occur through our choices to eat food that is sustainably produced, and to wear clothes that that are not made through exploitative labour.

INGOs

There are, broadly speaking, two types of global civil society. First, there are **international non-governmental organizations (INGOs)** with a global or international frame of reference for their actions and goals. INGOs deal with human rights and environmental and humanitarian disaster relief. The Campaign for Nuclear Disarmament, Greenpeace, Amnesty International and Oxfam are all examples. INGOs are semi-bureaucratic institutions that engage in building public support over a long period of time. They establish long-term relationships with governments or companies with whom they try to create policy change, getting states to conform to global human rights norms or encouraging multinational companies to embrace cleaner, renewable energy sources.

AMNESTY COMBINES THE KNOWLEDGE AND REPUTATION OF AN INTERNATIONAL ORGANIZATION WITH THE POWER OF MILLIONS OF VOICES, LIKE MINE.

Global Social Movements

A second type of global civil society is the social movement. Social movements are engaged in sustained mobilization for political ends: they are based on people power, are non-hierarchical, have shared beliefs and solidarity, and use protest tactics.

Grassroots movements are global because they operate and enjoy support in many countries. Global citizen action can take the form of consumer boycotts in wealthier nations in support of people in poorer nations. It can also be when movements in Western countries are inspired by the actions of movements in the so-called "Global South". For example, the Arab Spring has been a major influence on the global Occupy movement.

A key tool for the development of global civil society is social media. Social networking is a powerful way in which activists from across the globe can spread ideas and debates, and even the movement itself, across national borders to influence public opinion.

For example, Occupy Wall Street, a movement that began in New York City in 2011 to protest against social and economic inequalities, spread to include networked protests in over 1,000 cities across the globe.

Global Change?

Does global civil society seriously change the character of globalization? Direct change is always hard to measure since these movements do not run for political office. From a sociological point of view, however, it could be argued that these movements make an impact in various ways.

I'M MORE **AWARE** OF IMPORTANT ISSUES AND HOW THEY AFFECT MY LIFE.

THEY CHANGE THE WAY I **THINK** AND **TALK** ABOUT THE ISSUE...

... AND THEY FORCE GOVERNMENTS AND POLITICAL PARTIES TO **CHANGE** POLICY.

Social Movements

We know about the power of global social movements, but it is important to recognize that social movements existed long before globalization. Sociologists have studied social movements because they are both key indicators of social change as well as the engine of transformation within societies.

Anthony Giddens

SOCIAL MOVEMENTS ARE A COLLECTIVE ATTEMPT TO FURTHER A COMMON INTEREST OR SECURE A COMMON GOAL THROUGH COLLECTIVE ACTION OUTSIDE THE SPHERE OF ESTABLISHED INSTITUTIONS.

Social movements represent groups of people trying to change a specific aspect of society that they see as being unfair to them. Examples of renowned social movements include feminist, gay rights, animal rights, African-American civil rights, and the "green movement".

WHY HAVE STATES OVER THE PAST 100 YEARS INTRODUCED VOTING RIGHTS FOR WOMEN OR RECOGNIZED MARRIAGE EQUALITY FOR SEXUAL MINORITIES?

BECAUSE OF SOCIAL MOVEMENTS!

Old vs New Social Movements

A debate within sociology is the extent to which it is possible to distinguish "old" from "new" social movements. The Italian sociologist **Alberto Melucci** (1943–2001) argued that there are not only clear differences between old and new social movements, but that these distinctions are a product of social change.

Preceding generations of collective action largely focused on industrial workers demanding increased rights and wages. Another, related type of old social movement sought to gain citizenship rights and equality within the state. For instance, the suffragette movement demanded voting rights for women and the civil rights movement called for equal citizenship for African Americans.

Post-Materialism

Melucci claimed that Western societies have experienced tremendous social change since the 1960s. We now live in a post-industrial society, and this affects our values and priorities. Melucci drew upon the work of another sociologist, **Ronald Inglehart** (b.1934), who claimed that individuals rank goals in hierarchical order.

When we experience economic scarcities and insecurity, we emphasize and prioritize material needs, like financial issues, a strong national defence, and law and order. If our material needs are satisfied, we place a priority on values such as self-expression, quality of life and belonging. These are post-material values. The more prosperous a democratic society is, the more likely it is to emphasize post-materialism. Post-material values include a desire for personal empowerment, liberty and even a clean environment.

Post-material values

I JUST WANT TO KEEP A ROOF OVER MY FAMILY'S HEADS AND FOOD ON THE TABLE.

Material values

I'M LOOKING FOR A JOB THAT'S CREATIVE AND OFFERS GOOD WORK/LIFE BALANCE.

New Social Movements

Melucci argued that old social movements reflect a society characterized by material values. However, since the end of WWII, social movements are driven by post-material priorities.

NEW SOCIAL MOVEMENTS FOCUS ON INDIVIDUAL IMPROVEMENT, PERSONAL FREEDOM, CITIZEN INPUT IN GOVERNMENT DECISIONS, THE IDEAL OF A SOCIETY BASED ON HUMANISM AND MAINTAINING A CLEAN AND HEALTHY ENVIRONMENT.

Alberto Melucci

The membership of new social movements is mainly from the middle class, although their politics goes beyond left or right.

While sexuality was once seen as a private issue, some lesbian, gay, bisexual, transgender and queer (LGBTQ) movements have made it public by demanding, among other things, an end to discrimination by businesses and employers, and marriage equality.

Animal rights protestors make clothes and fashion into political issues, questioning not only the personal ethics of wearing animal products but also the broader social ethics involved with rearing and producing fur, leather and wool products.

Jürgen Habermas (b. 1929) provides an important contribution to the analysis of old and new social movements. Habermas distinguishes between old and new social movements based on both the conflicts they organize around and whether they seek or resist integration into what he calls the "system". First, in industrial, capitalist society, the "capital–labour" struggles of the labour movement provided the main battle line. Habermas claims that the labour movement has become institutionalized into trade unions and political parties: conflicts between capital and labour are advanced and fought through legal and political channels.

OLD SOCIAL MOVEMENTS PURSUE THEIR OBJECTIVES WITHIN THE POLITICAL SYSTEM. ONCE MOVEMENTS ARE LOCATED *WITHIN* THE SYSTEM, THEY LOSE MUCH OF THEIR POTENTIAL TO STIMULATE RADICAL CHANGE.

Jürgen Habermas

Lifeworld and System

New social movements remain outside of the political system. Their main conflict is to reject what Habermas calls the "colonization of the lifeworld": the intervention of the bureaucratic state and economy into areas of social life once restricted to the private sphere.

> "LIFEWORLD" IS THE SHARED MEANINGS THAT ALLOW CITIZENS TO COOPERATE AND CREATE SOCIAL ACTION.

The lifeworld for individuals is acquired through social institutions, such as the family, church, school and community. Habermas claims that our lifeworld has been negatively disrupted in contemporary society. The extension of a complex economic and bureaucratic system into all areas of everyday social life has created a crisis of legitimacy.

> CITIZENS NO LONGER BELIEVE THAT STATE AND ECONOMIC INSTITUTIONS ARE ACTING ON BEHALF OF OUR BEST INTERESTS.

Is this distinction between new and old social movements valid? **Craig Calhoun** (b.1952) argues that the analytical separation between old and new movements is unfounded.

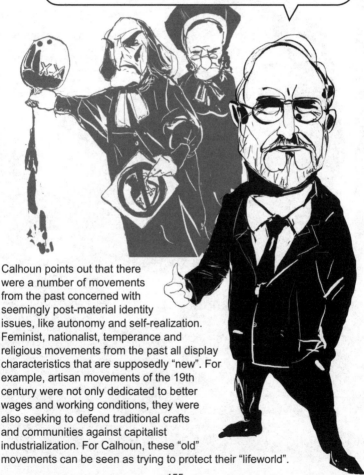

MANY OF THE FEATURES SAID TO BE INDICATIVE OF THE NOVELTY OF CONTEMPORARY MOVEMENTS ARE EVIDENT IN SOME SOCIAL MOVEMENTS FROM AS EARLY AS THE 18TH AND 19TH CENTURIES.

Calhoun points out that there were a number of movements from the past concerned with seemingly post-material identity issues, like autonomy and self-realization. Feminist, nationalist, temperance and religious movements from the past all display characteristics that are supposedly "new". For example, artisan movements of the 19th century were not only dedicated to better wages and working conditions, they were also seeking to defend traditional crafts and communities against capitalist industrialization. For Calhoun, these "old" movements can be seen as trying to protect their "lifeworld".

A different way to examine the apparent newness of contemporary movements is to ask whether they possess any "old" characteristics. Do contemporary movements continue to engage in conflicts over material issues and class struggle? Some contemporary movements appear to be located in conflicts that have elements of both the old and the new.

CONTEMPORARY ANTI-CORPORATE AND GLOBAL MOVEMENTS LIKE ANONYMOUS WRAP CONFLICTS ABOUT CAPITALIST PRODUCTION AND DISTRIBUTION OVER ISSUES OF CULTURE, IDENTITY AND LIFESTYLE.

Nations and Nationalism

We often take for granted that it is natural to divide the world up into nations. Sociologists debate the extent to which nations can be seen as either ancient or modern. Sociologists also debate the role of nations in a globalized world in which borders and boundaries appear increasingly porous.

Primordialism

Are nations natural structures in which members share an ethnic culture and history? Primordialism is the idea that nations are made up of ethnic groups who have common blood ties, kinship, racial features and culture. It views nations as ancient structures. **Pierre L. van den Berghe** (b.1933) put forward a sociobiological explanation for nations. He argued that members of ethnic groups are inclined to cooperate because of their "kinship networks". Nations emerge out of the desire of the ethnic group to protect itself. They have always been around, as they serve a core need of humans to band together based on a common ethnic identity.

Ethnic vs Civic Nationalism

Primordialism is closely related to ethnic nationalism, the idea that only those who belong to the ethnic group can be part of the nation. Ethnic nationalism is very dangerous as it can be used to justify violence against non-ethnic members of the nation.

ETHNIC NATIONALISM IS OFTEN RIGHT-WING, XENOPHOBIC AND EXTREMELY EXCLUSIVIST.

Pierre L. van den Berghe

A contrasting approach to imagining the nation is civic nationalism. Civic nationalism treats all citizens fairly and does not discriminate on the criteria of race and ethnicity.

CIVIC NATIONALISM IS INCLUSIVE AND LIBERAL. ANYBODY CAN BECOME PART OF THE NATION, AS LONG AS THEY POSSESS CITIZENSHIP.

Boundary Maintenance

Few sociologists would agree with the primordialist position, which assumes that ethnic groups are natural entities that share blood and DNA. Most sociologists would concur that that ethnicity and nationalism are sociologically constructed concepts. The constructivist position states that there are no inherent biological or genetic traits that mark out ethnic groups. **Fredrik Barth** (1928–2016) argues that we should not understand ethnic groups as biologically self-perpetuating, as having clear territorial boundaries or objective cultural traits. Instead, ethnic groups maintain and distinguish themselves through boundary construction and maintenance. They define their identity in opposition to other ethnic groups. Ethnic groups are socially constructed.

PEOPLE CAN, UNDER CERTAIN CONDITIONS, CHANGE THEIR ETHNIC IDENTITY, AND ETHNIC GROUPS CAN CHANGE OR EVEN SLOWLY VANISH OVER TIME. BOUNDARY CONSTRUCTION IS A PROCESS OF SOCIAL INTERACTION BETWEEN GROUPS.

Fredrik Barth

IT'S THEM OR US.

Modernism

If ethnic groups are socially constructed, then **Ernest Gellner** (1925–95) claimed that the same could be said about nations. Nationalism is an inevitable product of modern society.

According to Gellner, pre-modern society – characterized by mass illiteracy and low levels of population movement for the rural population – did not require nation-states.

The arrival of modern industrial society entailed massive social transformation, new forms of social stratification and individualism. Nationalism, then, serves a key function in modern society; it is invented as a means to unify the population.

> IN PRE-MODERN SOCIETY, NATIONS DO NOT NEED TO EXIST AND INDIVIDUALS DO NOT NEED A NATIONALITY. NATIONALISM INVENTS NATIONS WHERE THEY DID NOT EXIST BEFORE.

Ernest Gellner

The modern state lacks a strong connection to its population; it needs to instil a sense of the legitimacy of its rule. So, the state cultivates loyalty by creating the idea of the nation with which all members must identify.

Nationalism takes root through processes of state centralization and standardization. National identity is disseminated and perpetuated via the schooling system throughout the state. The history curriculum is standardized so that every child in the nation can learn of the great deeds of national heroes, kings and queens.

NATIONAL FLAGS, CEREMONIES AND NATIONAL ANTHEMS ARE INVENTED TO CULTIVATE THE PUBLIC'S LOYALTY TO THE STATE. SCHOOLS TURN CHILDREN INTO PATRIOTS AND CITIZENS LOYAL TO THE STATE.

Imagined Communities

Benedict Anderson (1936–2016) agreed with Gellner about the invented nature of the nation, but he pointed specifically to the development of print and mass media as key to the development of nationalism. Ideas about the nation are distributed by national newspapers and by popular literature; these print media, particularly newspapers, allowed for a consensus of opinion to be disseminated about national identity. Individuals from different regions of the state that were once disconnected from one another suddenly feel a sense of common national belonging.

Ethno-Symbolism

Anthony D. Smith (1939–2016) claimed that modernists, like Gellner and Anderson, overemphasize the constructed character of nations. Smith argued that while nation-states are relatively modern constructions, nations are much older. In other words, the idea of a national identity has long existed, but nation-states have only existed since the end of the 18th century.

Smith noted that, in order to create new nation-states, state-builders have often drawn on existing ethnic-national traditions, customs, identities and rituals. Smith called this "ethno-symbolism". Nationalists utilize a battery of myths, memories, values and symbols that are meant to represent the timelessness of the nation.

NATIONALISTS DEPLOY FLAGS, RESURRECT ANCIENT HEROES, STORIES, SONGS AND IMAGES FROM THE PAST TO MAKE IT SEEM THAT THE NATION HAS ALWAYS ENDURED.

Anthony D. Smith

The ethno-symbolist position provides an uneasy reconciliation of the modernist vs primordialist debate: Smith agreed that nation-states are a modern invention, but argued they aren't simply summoned out of thin air to cope with the challenges of industrial society. State-builders need to draw on existing national traditions.

Smith also criticized modernism for its failure to address the passion of nationalism. It cannot answer the question: why die for the nation? For Smith, the answer lies in the "sacred community" of shared memories and ancestry. For people to invest a deep sense of belonging to the nation, they are required to subscribe to the feeling that the nation is a primordial force of nature. Nationalists encourage primordialist stirrings among the population by using apparently ancient national symbols and myths. The myth of the "chosen people" is a particularly powerful narrative.

Globalization and Nationalism

How have nations and nationalism responded to globalization?
Eric Hobsbawm (1917–2012) claimed that the age of nationalism is coming to end. Nationalism was constructed to suit an earlier historical period dominated by industrialization and print technology. It no longer serves a necessary function in a post-industrial society and highly globalized economy.

It is said that the institution of the nation-state is becoming less important. Nation-states have less power over economic decisions as they are integrated into a global economy led by multinational corporations. Nation-states have less power over political decisions as many powers are devolved to trans-state organizations, like the EU, UN, World Bank and NATO. Our cultural choices are also globalized.

Eric Hobsbawm

Yet nationalism has not gone away. Since the end of the Cold War in 1991, there have been a number of devastating nationalist conflicts around the world, such as in the former Yugoslavia and Ukraine. Anthony D. Smith didn't think that nations had been transcended in the global era. The current wave of nationalism in various parts of the world testifies to the enduring nature of the national idea and the way in which it responds to some deep-seated human need. Anthony Giddens notes the "revival of local nationalisms" that emerges in response to globalizing tendencies. Therein lies a paradox.

Anthony D. Smith

SMALL NATIONS ARE NEEDED TO HELP PEOPLE TAKE BACK CONTROL OF POLITICAL AND ECONOMIC DECISIONS.

THE NATION-STATE ENDURES IN A GLOBALIZED WORLD.

Manuel Castells (b.1942) has a different answer to the question of the relationship between globalization and nationalism. He interprets the new nationalism as a defensive reaction to globalization. The economic, social and cultural influences of globalization destroy traditional forms of social and political association; they dissolve boundaries and cause instability and uncertainty about the future.

Nationalism represents an attempt by social groups to defend themselves from these threats. New nationalism takes the appearance of old forms of ethnic nationalism which are xenophobic and exclusivist.

Manuel Castells

THE WHIRLWIND OF GLOBALIZATION IS TRIGGERING DEFENSIVE REACTIONS AROUND THE WORLD, OFTEN ORGANIZED AROUND THE PRINCIPLE OF NATIONAL AND TERRITORIAL IDENTITY.

Rocking the World?

Well, you might reflect, sociology may be a clever enterprise when it comes to explaining our world, but does it really change anything? You look around and quite reasonably conclude that we still live in a world marked by clear inequalities between individuals and groups. We still have patriarchy, homophobia, economic exploitation, xenophobia and racism. Surely, this shows that sociology is rather powerless when it comes to making our societies less defined by inequality?

How do we assess the "outcomes" of a discipline like sociology which has been around for over a hundred years? This question is further complicated by the fact that there is little consensus among sociologists about what type of society they would like to see.

HOW DO WE DEMONSTRATE THAT SOCIOLOGY HAS CONSEQUENCES FOR PUBLIC POLICIES AND IDEAS THAT GENERATE CHANGE FOR THE BETTER?

In this regard, we could respond by pointing out that some sociological ideas have been adopted by governments. For example, Anthony Giddens worked closely with the British government in the late 1990s on policies related to social justice. Sociologists are also often courted by the media to analyse various social problems and issues, which may help the public to better understand and react to them.

Searching for clear evidence of sociology's impact on government policy risks narrowing the discipline's impact. Sociologist **Michael Burawoy** (b. 1947) argues an alternative way to understand sociology's relevance is to see it as a mirror, where we can look at ourselves and our society.

This mirror is often obscured from our view, or we are unable to make out the image reflected back to us. In recognizing our image, we question whether we like it and ask how we can change it for the better.

Bibliography

Ang, I. (2013) *Watching* Dallas*: Soap opera and the melodramatic imagination*. Routledge.

Beck, U. (1992) *Risk Society: Towards a new modernity* (Vol. 17). Sage.

Butler, J. (2011) *Gender Trouble: Feminism and the subversion of identity*. Routledge.

Bourdieu, P. (1984) *Distinction: A social critique of the judgement of taste*. Harvard University Press.

Connell, R.W. (2005) *Masculinities*. University of California Press.

Du Bois, W.E.B., & Edwards, B.H. (2007) *The Souls of Black Folk*. Oxford University Press.

Durkheim, E., & Giddens, A. (1972) *Emile Durkheim: Selected writings*. Cambridge University Press.

Gellner, E. (2008) *Nations and Nationalism*. Cornell University Press.

Foucault, M. (1980) *Power/Knowledge: Selected interviews and other writings, 1972–1977*. Pantheon.

Foucault, M. (2012) *The History of Sexuality, Vol. 2: The use of pleasure*. Vintage.

Fulcher, J., & Scott, J. (2003) *Sociology*. Oxford University Press.

Gilroy, P. (2013). *There Ain't No Black in the Union Jack*. Routledge.

Goffman, E. (1978) *The Presentation of Self in Everyday Life*. Harmondsworth.

Harvey, D. (1989) *The Condition of Postmodernity: An enquiry into the origins of cultural change*. John Wiley & Sons.

Habermas, J. (1991) *The Structural Transformation of the Public Sphere: An inquiry into a category of bourgeois society*. MIT Press.

Hochschild, A.R. (2003) *The Managed Heart: Commercialization of human feeling*. University of California Press.

Inglehart, R. (2015) *The Silent Revolution: Changing values and political styles among Western publics*. Princeton University Press.

Lyon, D. (2001) *Surveillance Society: Monitoring everyday life*. McGraw-Hill Education (UK).

Lyotard, J.F. (1984) *The Postmodern Condition: A report on knowledge* (Vol. 10). University of Minnesota Press.

Macionis, J.J., & Plummer, K. (2005) *Sociology: A global introduction*. Pearson Education.

Mills, C.W. (2000) *The Sociological Imagination*. Oxford University Press.

Modood, T. (2013) *Multiculturalism*. John Wiley & Sons.

Ritzer, G. (2011) *The McDonaldization of Society*. Pine Forge Press.

Robertson, R. (1992). *Globalization: Social theory and global culture* (Vol. 16). Sage.

Wallerstein, I.M. (2004). *World-Systems Analysis: An introduction*. Duke University Press.

Weber, M. (2002). *The Protestant Ethic and the Spirit of Capitalism: And other writings*. Penguin.

About the Creators

John Nagle is a lecturer at the University of Aberdeen, where he researches conflict and peace processes, multiculturalism and social movements. His work is widely published in the academic and popular press, and he has provided research consultancy for both the media and international public policy bodies.

Piero is an illustrator, artist and graphic designer whose work has been included in the Royal College of Art in London. He has illustrated many Introducing titles.

Index